Famous Pistols and Hand Guns

General Editor

A. J. R. Cormack

Published by
PROFILE PUBLICATIONS LTD.
Windsor, Berkshire, England.

© *Profile Publications Ltd.* 1977

ISBN 0 214 20320 4

First published in 1977 by
PROFILE PUBLICATIONS LIMITED
Dial House, Park St, Windsor, Berkshire, England

Printed in England by
GPS (Print) Limited

Contents

Acknowledgements

The author would like to thank the following for their help without which this volume would not have been possible. Herb Woodend of the Pattern Room at Enfield, the manufacturer's Astra, Beretta, FN, Colt, Walther and Webley, R. Shattuck and W. H. Buxton.

Foreword

This volume contains a collection of informed histories of pistols and handguns that have made their mark on the battlefields, streets, and target ranges of the world. All have their staunchest admirers, all have their place in the development of the handgun.

The Luger has been the soldier's weapon, the enthusiast's pistol and the thriller writer's friend for seventy years. This is the story of the Luger from the large complicated Borchardt of the 1890's to the new Mauser production of the present day. Included is a list compiled by Mr R. Shattuck of all variants.

The Mauser 1898 may never have achieved the status of a military success but the ugly Broomhandle has been carried through numerous wars. The famous such as Sir Winston Churchill have had it with them when most needed. It owes nothing to the age of mass production and all to the age of the craftsman.

The best known of the Walther range, the P38, PP and PPK have all made their name, the P38 as the successor to the Luger, the PP and PPK in the hands of the soldier, police and civilian. The little known Models 1 to 9 are described in detail. The P38 is still in production as the P1 as are its smaller companions the PP and PPK, surely testimony enough.

When the great John Moses Browning designed the Model 1900 Colt, he could hardly have thought that its derivative the Colt 1911 would with little or no modification be still in production and front line service sixty years after its announcement. With the introduction of the '70 series, Colt prove that this old war horse will not lie down and die.

The histories of JM Browning, FN, and the automatic pistol are unable to be separated. The first large scale production of an automatic pistol was the FN produced, Browning designed Model 1900. Design after design followed to be finalised after Brownings death with the Browning Hi-Power. The Hi-Power is still the standard side arm of many armies and a popular pistol on the target-range.

Perhaps better known for their revolvers Webley and Scott also produced a number of very successful automatic pistols. The massive .455 Model 1912 with its square no nonsense looks served Britain in the First WW and the Model 1913 .32 was carried in cases of emergency by the police. The unusual semi-automatic single shot is detailed along with the pistol that could have equipped the British Army.

With the firm of Beretta the customer comes first and first class quality is normal. Possibly the reason is that the firm, founded in 1680 by the Beretta family is still in 1976 under their direct control. The Model 1934 has equipped the Italian forces from its inception to this day. It and the other automatic pistols are all detailed in this section.

If any firm has shown that Spanish firearms can compete with the best in the world, Astra must be a prime candidate. The resurgence of the name with the introduction of a first class range of revolvers is more than justified by their quality. From the Campogiro of 1913 the firm has produced automatic pistols that have equipped armies in France, Germany and Spain. All these pistols are described along with such presentation weapons as that of American President Johnson.

A. J. R. CORMACK

Index

Rare Krieghoff marked, DWM
manufactured Luger   (*R. Shattuck*)

The Luger
by A. J. R. Cormack

Of all the firearms in history the Luger must surely
be the pistol about which there has been more
discussion and whose name is better known than
any other. Even the years from 1943 to 1970 when it
was out of production did not eclipse its fame.
Partially this was because A. F. Stoeger (who own
the trade-name 'Luger' in the United States) make
one 'lookalike' model while Erma make another and
thus the Luger image was maintained. But even
more it is because of the mystique that the Luger
acquired during its golden years. And those years
may well return. After a break since 1943 Mauser
have resumed Luger production. It looks as though
the Luger refuses to give way to its better and
cheaper modern rivals. Indeed, such is the strength
of the Luger's hold that even the word 'better' will be
strongly denied by the many dedicated enthusiasts
of this weapon.

History
The Luger history ranges from the invention of the
toggle action by Sir Hiram Maxim, though its
modification into pistol application by Hugo
Borchardt, and finally into the creation of a practical
military side-arm by George Luger.
Hugo Borchardt was a citizen of the United States,
and during the time that he worked for Winchester
and Sharps, he took out a number of patents. His
real contributions to small arms design were the
Sharps-Borchardt single shot rifle and the little-
known but interesting Winchester experimental
revolvers, of which he designed nine altogether,
incorporating such features as solid frames, side-
break loading, and, on one, a bottle-necked
cartridge. Borchardt moved first from the United
States to the Budapest State Arsenal, where he was
the Director, and then, more importantly for the

A current Mauser produced Luger
calibre 7·65 with a 4in barrel.
Right side   (*Interarms*)

Below: Notice the Interarms banner which
indicates their interest in marketing this
weapon   (*Interarms*)

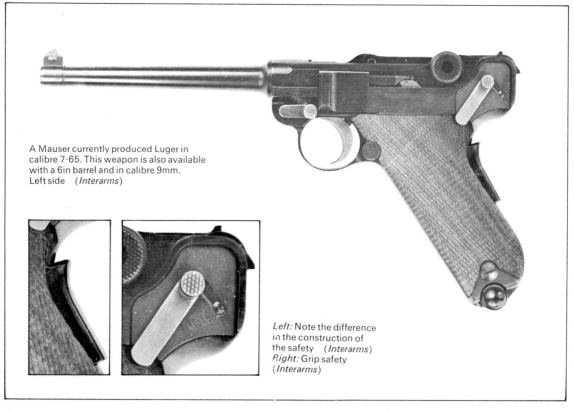

A Mauser currently produced Luger in
calibre 7·65. This weapon is also available
with a 6in barrel and in calibre 9mm.
Left side   (*Interarms*)

Left: Note the difference
in the construction of
the safety   (*Interarms*)
Right: Grip safety
(*Interarms*)

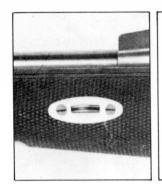

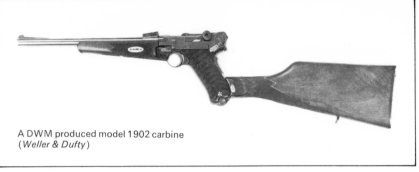

A DWM produced model 1902 carbine
(*Weller & Dufty*)

future of firearms, to Ludwig Loewe of Berlin. It was during his time here that he designed the forerunner of the Luger.

Borchardt

Although it was the first application to a pistol, the toggle action used by Borchardt was not in itself new, as Sir Hiram Maxim had used it on a number of his designs. The original patent number 18774 was taken out by Borchardt on 6 October 1893. The Borchardt was the first auto-pistol produced in any number, but it was not altogether practical, as it weighed $2\frac{1}{2}$lb and even without the shoulder stock was 15in. long. It was an extremely accurate weapon, especially when employed as a carbine with the shoulder stock fitted. The author has found the Borchardt to be a comfortable weapon to handle but, with the predominance of the weight on the back of the gun caused by the fitting of the recoil spring at that point, it has a tendency to sit back muzzle light when pointed.

Although the weapon has all that is necessary for a

Below right: The toggle lock which was also used on the early Lugers
Below left: Patent markings

A 1906 Model Luger supplied to the Russian government   (*R. Shattuck*)
Below right: Safety markings in Russian script
Below left: The Russian crest of crossed Mosin Nagant rifles

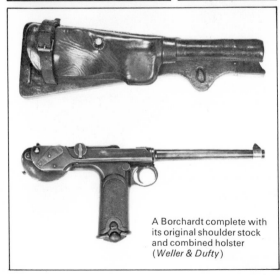

A Borchardt complete with its original shoulder stock and combined holster
(*Weller & Dufty*)

successful automatic pistol, having features such as a detachable magazine, its fragility from a combat point of view and its non-acceptance by the military, were probably the reasons for its poor sales. Only some 3000 were produced between 1893 and 1899. During production Ludwig Loewe and Metallpateronenfabrik amalgamated to form Deutsche Waffen und Munitionsfabriken (DWM) where the last of the Borchardts were manufactured. The cartridge was to outlast the pistol, as the 7·63 Mauser chambered a bottle-necked dimen-sionally exact copy, but with a considerably heavier loading. The Mauser round was in turn used by the Soviet Forces where it was known as the Tokarev 7·62. The Borchardt should be regarded as a collector's piece but, if any attempt is made to fire it, the above must be remembered, as Mauser or Tokarev ammunition could well result in a damaged

3

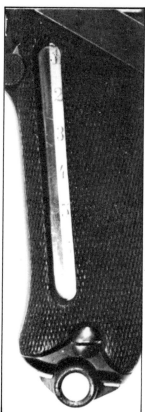

A model 1902 Luger supplied to the American government with the Powel cartridge counter   (*R. Shattuck*)
Right: The Powel cartridge counter

gun. True Borchardt ammunition is extremely difficult to identify unless the original packing is available.

Transition

George Luger was employed as a weapon salesman and it is probable that the ideas for the transition from Borchardt to Luger began during his demonstrations of the Borchardt. The spelling of Luger has been doubted by some historians but it is clear from his signature on the patent documents that the above is correct. In 1897 Luger visited the United States for a demonstration at Springfield Armoury and during his stay in the United States he took out a number of patents for improvements on automatic pistols. Finally, in 1900, Luger took out a very long and specifically detailed patent in Great Britain, followed by a similar one in the United States, in 1904. Luger's detailed patent probably stemmed from the fact that the Luger bore a close resemblance to the Borchardt ! Reports varied as to whether Luger and Borchardt were on friendly terms but, as rumour has it that Luger was ordered to perfect Borchardt's design when the latter refused, one can understand

A rare Mauser prototype Luger
(*R. Shattuck*)

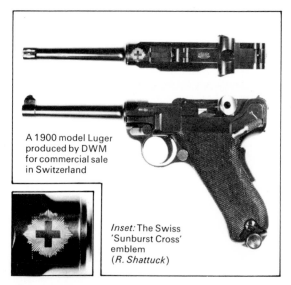

A 1900 model Luger produced by DWM for commercial sale in Switzerland

Inset: The Swiss 'Sunburst Cross' emblem
(*R. Shattuck*)

An 8″ BARREL Luger shown field-stripped. Notice the detached side plate and the recoil spring hook at the rear of the slide. *Author.*

The toggle marking shows a Mauser banner type marking. The extractor is at the front of the toggle and has the part serial number 30. *Lowland Brigade Depot.*

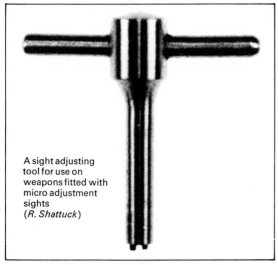

A sight adjusting tool for use on weapons fitted with micro adjustment sights (*R. Shattuck*)

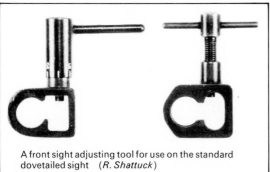

A front sight adjusting tool for use on the standard dovetailed sight (*R. Shattuck*)

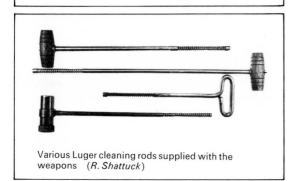

Various Luger cleaning rods supplied with the weapons   (*R. Shattuck*)

any hostility. The new pistol was submitted to the Swiss for trial in 1898 and in a further modified form in 1899. At this time it was named the Borchardt-Luger. Possibly only 10 of these transitional weapons were ever manufactured.

The Luger Model 1900

The Swiss were the first to order the Luger in quantity when 3000 were made for them by the DWM combine for millitary use and some 2000 for commercial sale. In 1901 the United States Government ordered 1000 for testing by its troops, and commercial concerns ordered some 10,000 more. As well as this order, a number of contract weapons were built for the Bulgarian Government. All these weapons feature a toggle lock which was used as an extra precaution against the toggle breaking too soon when the weapon was fired.

All model 1900 Lugers are chambered for the 7·65mm Luger round.

A group of Waffen SS grenadiers one of whom is holding a Luger   (*IWM*)

Model 1902

Although relatively few of this model were manufactured it is famous because it was the first to be chambered for 9mm parabellum. The United States continued to order small quantities for testing and for commercial sale. The Luger carbine also appeared for the first time as a commercial weapon.

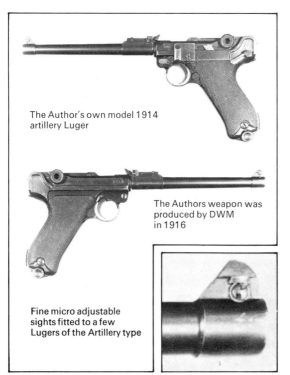

The Author's own model 1914 artillery Luger

The Authors weapon was produced by DWM in 1916

Fine micro adjustable sights fitted to a few Lugers of the Artillery type

A model 1914 artillery Luger with an early type wooden base magazine

The classic lines of the Luger are well illustrated by this view

There were some 2500 manufactured, a great number of which were exported to the United States and Great Britain. The cartridge used in the carbine was an uprated one and because it is not safe in a standard pistol, the case is painted black.

Model 1903 and 1904 Navy

These weapons were only manufactured in very small quantities, 50 of the 1903 commercial and just over 1000 of the 1904 Navy. The Navy weapon has a 6in. barrel and is chambered for 9mm parabellum, and the commercial has a 4in. barrel in 7·65mm parabellum. These weapons can be considered as transitional between the 'old' and 'new' models. Their use by the German Navy was the first time that the weapon had been accepted by the military in Germany.

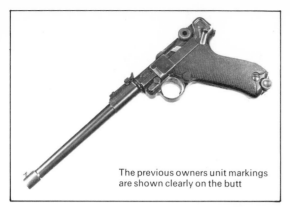
The previous owners unit markings are shown clearly on the butt

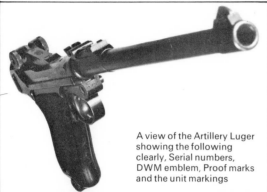
A view of the Artillery Luger showing the following clearly, Serial numbers, DWM emblem, Proof marks and the unit markings

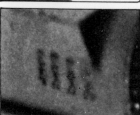

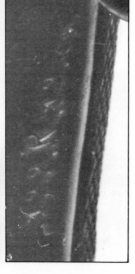

The side plate with the demounting lever in the stripping position. This enables the weapon to be field stripped. The Serial number is clearly visible as well as the habit of using the last two digits on each major part of the weapon

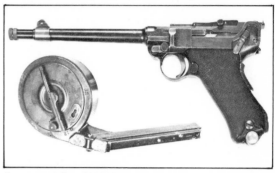
A commercially sold 1906 Luger fitted with the rare Erma ·22 conversion. Note the early type of Snail Drum magazine
Below left: The conversion toggle which enables the weapon to use ·22 long rifle ammunition
Below right: The conversion barrel held in place concentrically with the standard one by the nut   (*Weller & Dufty*)

The Old and New Models

The external differences between the two weapons are the dished toggle grips on the old model and the flat toggle grips on the new. Also most old models were fitted with the toggle lock which held the toggle closed during the initial recoil period until the action was opened under the influence of the cams. This feature was dropped as it was found unnecessary. There is a difference in the dimensions of the frame and the receiver, and also in the manufacture of the barrels, thus making the old and new models non-interchangeable. The greatest difference, however, is the use of a coil spring for the recoil spring in the new model as compared to the leaf spring in the old model. This change was made owing to breakages occurring in the leaf type spring.

Model 1906

This, and all subsequent Luger models are called the 'new' models because they feature the recoil spring change and the other major design changes, changes which were the only ones in the Luger's production history.

The original Borchardt patent drawings. Notice the progressive development shown in this and the next illustrations

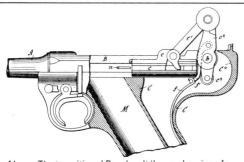

Above: The transitional Borchardt/Luger drawings for the patent by Luger

Below: The final patent drawings which show the early production leaf recoil spring

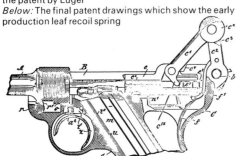

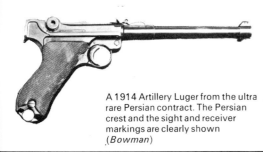

A 1914 Artillery Luger from the ultra rare Persian contract. The Persian crest and the sight and receiver markings are clearly shown *(Bowman)*

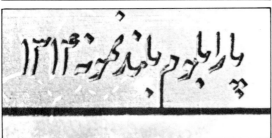

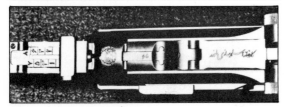

This model 1914 Artillery Luger has been engraved long after it left the factory *(Weller & Dufty)*

The German Navy ordered, in two lots, 24,000 of Model 1906 with a 6in. barrel. Once again a number of contract weapons were produced, in both calibres 7·65mm and 9mm, mainly for export to the United States but also in very small numbers, for commercial sale in France, and in larger numbers for sale in Switzerland. 4000 were produced for the Dutch Military ; 2000 for the Portuguese Navy ; 5000 for the Brazilian Government ; 1500 for the Bulgarian Government, and 1000 for the Russian Government.

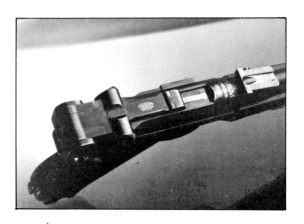

Above and below:
This 1902 model carbine has been finished as a presentation weapon. Such weapons are very rare and one can only wonder at the initial of the recipient *(R. Shattuck)*

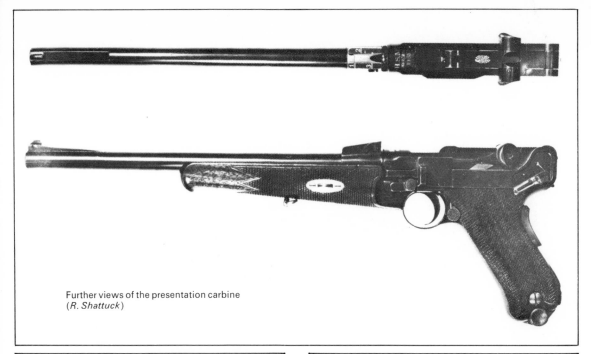

Further views of the presentation carbine
(*R. Shattuck*)

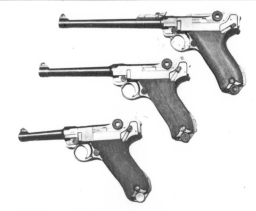

A clear view of the three main barrel lengths. Notice also the multi ringed magazine base used on some early weapons (*Thompson*)

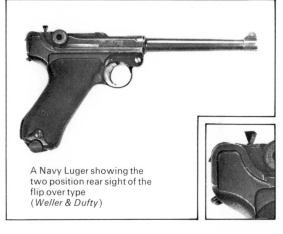

A Navy Luger showing the two position rear sight of the flip over type
(*Weller & Dufty*)

This is the standard 9mm 4in barrel weapon of the Second World War. The owner has the original holster which indicates by its markings that the weapon was used by a member of the SS (*Bowman*)

Model 1908

This was the first model to be accepted officially by the German Army and, as the Army designation was 'Pistol Model 1908', this gave rise to the standard nomenclature 'P.08'. (*Note:* Model P.38—Walther ; P.35 Radom). The German Navy also took 40,000 with a 6in. barrel. This weapon was very little changed from the previous model, except that the grip safety was deleted and the safety catch made to work in the opposite direction, thus making the weapon more satisfactory for military use as well as being easier to produce.

For the first time a manufacturer other than DWM produced the Luger, as a result of the licensing of the Royal Arsenal at Erfurt to produce weapons for the German Army. Many thousands were produced by both DWM and Erfurt. Once again a number of contract and commercial weapons were produced, some of which, unlike all other 1908 production, were in calibre 7·65 Luger with 4in. and 6in. barrels. One such contract was for the Bulgarian Government.

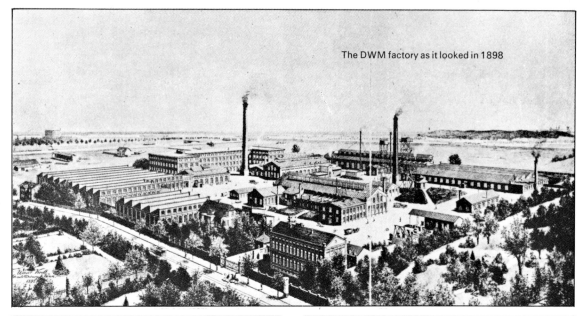

The DWM factory as it looked in 1898

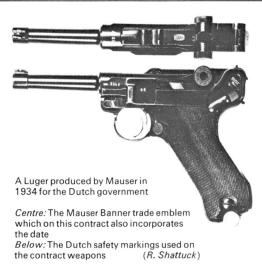

A Luger produced by Mauser in 1934 for the Dutch government

Centre: The Mauser Banner trade emblem which on this contract also incorporates the date
Below: The Dutch safety markings used on the contract weapons   (*R. Shattuck*)

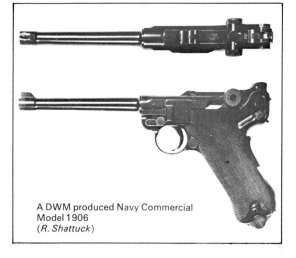

A DWM produced Navy Commercial Model 1906
(*R. Shattuck*)

Model 1914

The most commonly known Model 1914 is the so called 'Long Barrel Luger'. This was a built-up weapon, which had a special 8in. barrel fitted to a 1908 receiver. The gun was normally supplied with a shoulder stock and often with a 32 round drum magazine, nicknamed a 'snail drum'. It was also manufactured in two other barrel lengths, 4in. and 6in. Its production was carried out at both DWM and Erfurt where many thousands of 4in. and 8in. weapons were produced. All 1914 weapons were in calibre 9mm parabellum both military and commercial.

Notice the Krieghoff name
and the address
(*R. Shattuck*)

A 1935/37 manufactured
Krieghoff Commercial
(*R. Shattuck*)

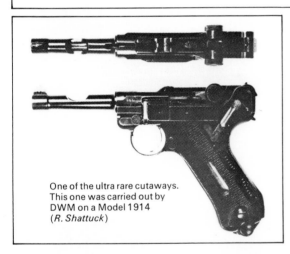

One of the ultra rare cutaways.
This one was carried out by
DWM on a Model 1914
(*R. Shattuck*)

A DWM Luger produced for the
American market. This weapon
is one of those ordered by
A. F. Stoeger
(*R. Shattuck*)

The markings which were part of the deal with DWM
(*R. Shattuck*)

Swiss Model 1924/29

This was the first Swiss manufactured Luger and was
a modified copy of the 1906 German model. The
weapons were manufactured by Waffenfabrik,
Berne, and in the later 1929 version both the grip
shape and the safety were altered to ease production.
The weapons were in 7·65 with 4¾in. barrels mainly
for military use but also later for commercial sale.
The Swiss designation for the Luger models is
Ordonnanzpistolen Mod 00-06-29.

Inter-War and World War II Lugers

After the end of the First World War and before the
commencement of the Nazi weapon build-up
before the Second World War, a number of military
and commercial, as well as contract weapons, were
produced from wartime weapons or manufactured
from scratch. In theory at least, under the Treaty of
Versailles, these weapons should had have a
maximum calibre of 8mm and a barrel of under
100mm. But there were many evasions of the regu-
lations. A number of weapons were in fact manu-

factured or reworked in 9mm parabellum with
barrels of 6 and 8in.
In 1922 Simpson and Co of Suhl were appointed
suppliers to the 100,000 man Reichswehr. Initially
the weapons were assembled from leftover parts
manufactured during World War I by Erfurt and
DWM. In 1930 Mauser began to assemble weapons
along with Simpson, and when Simpson ended
production in 1932 Mauser took over the bulk of the
Luger production.
The firm of Krieghoff also began assembly of leftover parts and at a later date parts purchased from
DWM who were once again manufacturing. It is

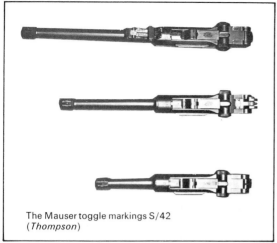

The Mauser toggle markings S/42
(*Thompson*)

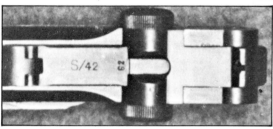

The latter type of Snail Drum Magazine showing
the loading lever in the open and closed positions
(*Lowland Brigade Depot*)

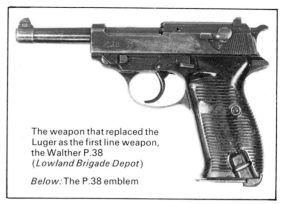

The weapon that replaced the
Luger as the first line weapon,
the Walther P.38
(*Lowland Brigade Depot*)

Below: The P.38 emblem

A view of the Author's Artillery Luger clearly showing the
date, sight micro adjuster, serial number and the proof marks

also probable that Krieghoff supplied weapons
produced by DWM but marked Krieghoff. Later,
along with Mauser, Krieghoff produced weapons of
their own, possibly at the old Simpson factory. DWM
were absorbed by Berlin Kartsruhn Industrie Werk
(BKIW) who in turn became part of Mauser in 1930.
A number of codes were used to conceal both the
number of weapons and their manufacturers.
Examples of these are 'S/42', '42' and 'byf' for
Mauser. This initially was to prevent the implement-
ation of the Treaty of Versailles but later became a
normal wartime procedure. There are also markings
to be found on the grip of the Luger. These are not

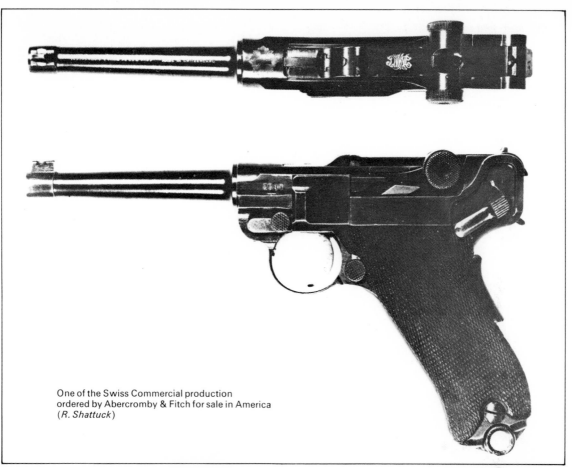

One of the Swiss Commercial production ordered by Abercromby & Fitch for sale in America (*R. Shattuck*)

Inset: The Portuguese Navy Markings

A model 1906 Luger supplied by DWM under contract to the Portuguese Navy (*R. Shattuck*)

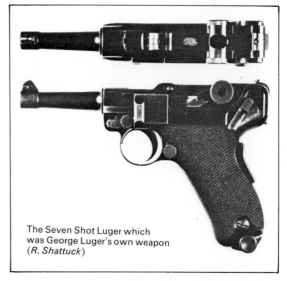

The Seven Shot Luger which was George Luger's own weapon (*R. Shattuck*)

manufacturers' markings but unit codes. Examples of these are HR for Husaren Regiment, POL for Poliziei Regiment. German Naval markings, for example, WH for Werft Hamburg, WB for Werft Bremen, WK for Werft Keil.

Because of the complexity of manufacture—both in time and labour—the main sidearm was changed to the Walther P.38 and Luger production ceased in 1943.

Some weapons have been found that were possibly assembled after the war for the Occupying Troops.

Vickers' Lugers
Although the facts of Vickers production have never been substantiated some conjecture is possible.
The Dutch had purchased a large number of Lugers in calibre 7·65mm from DWM but as a result of their experience in the First World War they felt the

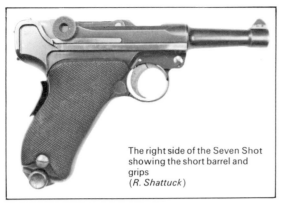

The right side of the Seven Shot showing the short barrel and grips
(R. Shattuck)

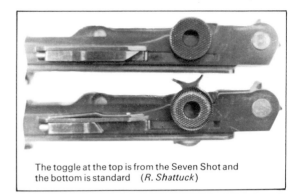

The toggle at the top is from the Seven Shot and the bottom is standard   (R. Shattuck)

The serial number and the GL monogram on the Seven Shot
(R. Shattuck)

A Luger Model 1900 supplied to Bulgaria under contract showing the Bulgarian markings
(R. Shattuck)

An American Eagle marked 1900 Model Luger supplied to America for commercial sale
(R. Shattuck)

The magazine on the left is from the Seven Shot and the standard on the right. Notice the difference in length (R. Shattuck)

weapon ought to have a calibre of 9mm. However, as the Treaty of Versailles forbade the Germans to manufacture 9mm weapons for export the Dutch had to look elsewhere. The only difference between the two calibres of weapon is the actual barrel and so Vickers, who obtained the contract, had only to

The Erfurt Mark of a Crown over the Name
(*Lowland Brigade Depot*)

A Mauser Test Weapon used for ammunition testing
with a removable barrel   (*R. Shattuck*)

One of the rare Spandau
Lugers of which only 100 were
made
(*R. Shattuck*)

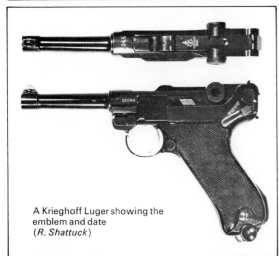

A Krieghoff Luger showing the
emblem and date
(*R. Shattuck*)

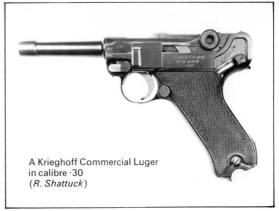

A Krieghoff Commercial Luger
in calibre ·30
(*R. Shattuck*)

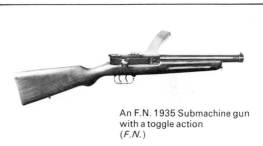

An F.N. 1935 Submachine gun
with a toggle action
(*F.N.*)

necessity of special jigs and tools etc. The logical conclusion is that, as DWM were once again producing weapons and were able to export parts legally, Vickers purchased part-machined Lugers with the exception of the barrel. They would then manufacture the barrel at Elswick and finish assembly of the weapons. Most of these are marked with the Royal Netherlands cypher, a Dutch crown above a W, and a number are reported to have had Japanese markings stamped on them at a later date. This would be explained by the Japanese capture of a large amount of military equipment when they over-ran the Dutch troops in the Far East in 1941-42.
It is interesting that the Dutch continued to use German produced Lugers in 9mm during 1936-40.

American Lugers—Commercial and Military
The American Luger is divided clearly into two categories, commercial and military.

Commercial
The sales of the Borchardt were handled by a New York cutlery dealer Herman Bocker & Co, but when DWM were formed they sent their own representative, Hans Tausher, to the United States to work in conjunction with Bocker & Co. Hans Tausher not only sold weapons to the retail outlets but he negotiated their sale to the American Army.
After World War I the firm of Hugo J. Panzer & Co of New York was licensed to sell or manufacture Luger pistols by the Government. But A. F. Stoeger was made an agent for the Luger by DWM. In the end, after numerous disagreements, H. J. Panzer & Co signed over all their rights to Stoeger. Stoeger continued to sell the Luger from 1921 up to the outbreak of World War II, and, as has been mentioned at the beginning of this Profile, now owns the

use a different barrel from the standard 7·65mm 1908. Because of wartime contracts and the post-war problems it is more than likely that the guns were not manufactured until the 1920s. It would seem probable that the full manufacture of 11,000 weapons would be uneconomic owing to the

trade name Luger in the United States. A. F. Stoeger's agreement with DWM was for Lugers to be supplied with the American Eagle mark in boxes marked with the name Stoeger. In 1931 when Mauser began production, Stoeger ordered all pistols supplied by them to be marked with the name A. F. Stoeger. Abercombie and Fitch of New York also imported a few weapons from Switzerland with $4\frac{3}{4}$in. barrels in both calibres.

Military
The United States decided to hold tests to find a suitable pistol for the Army and 1000 Lugers were ordered for the competition. These weapons are similar to the standard 1900 commercial production and are numbered between 6099 and 7098. Two shipments were received at Governor Island, New York and the weapons distributed to a number of military establishments for test. The predominant complaint from all the personnel testing the weapon was that a larger calibre than 7·65mm was desirable. Tausher proposed to exchange 50 of the smaller calibre pistols for a similar number of 9mm weapons. These weapons were to be fitted with a cartridge counting device designed by G. H. Powell. They were serial numbered 22401 up to 22450 and were delivered to New York on 6 May 1903. With the demand for a larger calibre, Luger was asked to

redesign the weapon to fire a ·45 calibre bullet. The American Frankford Arsenal supplied Luger with 5000 rounds of ·45 Colt automatic ammunition which Luger dismantled and, using the bullet and a modified 11mm Gergman case, manufactured the ·45 Luger cartridge. The gun, of which only two or three were made, was a very much modified 1906. This weapon, although performing very creditably in competition with others, was rejected and the ·45 Colt Automatic accepted instead. Correspondence discovered by Michael Reese II, a Luger expert, indicates that owing to the success of the pistol in Europe and the apparently delaying tactics employed by the American Government, DWM decided to supply no further weapons. The pistols were withdrawn by the United States Government in 1904 and in 1906 all serviceable weapons were auctioned off, most of them being purchased by Francis Bannerman & Co at $10.00 each.

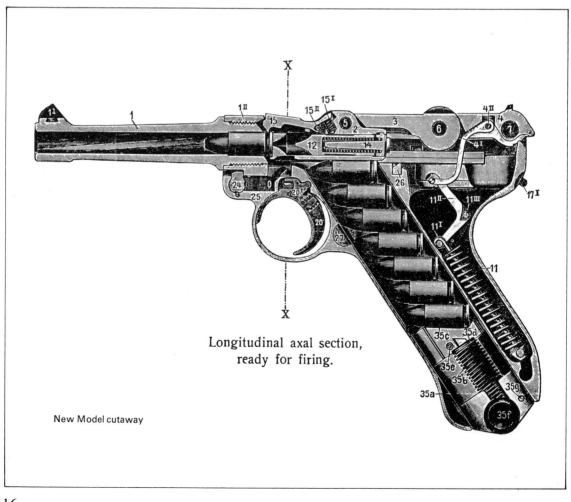

Longitudinal axal section, ready for firing.

New Model cutaway

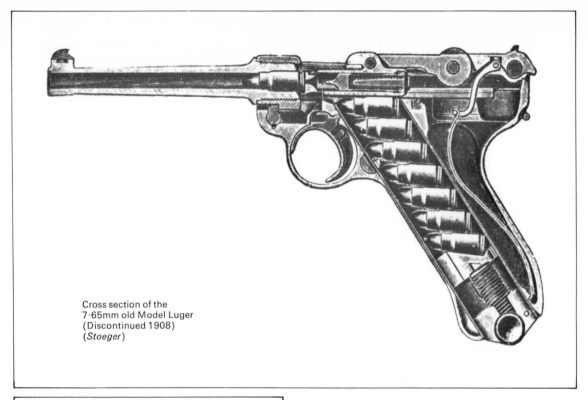

Cross section of the
7·65mm old Model Luger
(Discontinued 1908)
(*Stoeger*)

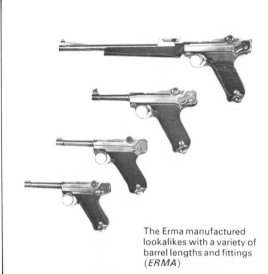

The Erma manufactured
lookalikes with a variety of
barrel lengths and fittings
(*ERMA*)

Miscellaneous Lugers and Accessories

Silencers—Attempts were made to manufacture a silencer but as had been discovered by experiments the standard 9mm parabellum round has too high a velocity to silence efficiently. The Germans therefore produced a special subsonic low velocity round which could be used single shot fashion from the Luger when it was fitted with a silencer. Very few were made which indicates a lack of success.

Fully Automatic Variant—Although it is probable that a number of attempts were made by a variety of firms to develop a fully automatic weapon, the first record of a patent is credited to a Mexican. No successful conversions were ever marketed. Waffenfabrik of Berne and FN of Belgium amongst others did manufacture submachine guns using the basic toggle action.

Seven Shot and Baby Models—The seven-shot weapon was built by George Luger for his personal use and indications are that it was probably produced around 1905 to 1910. The weapon has a $3\frac{1}{4}$in. barrel chambered for 9mm parabellum and a seven-shot magazine. The frame, grip and the toggle have all been modified. The weapon bears the GL hallmark which indicates George Luger's personal interest. This weapon is owned by Mr Ralph Shattuck of the U.S.A.
In all, four Baby Models were manufactured; two in 9mm Browning Short and two in ·32 ACP. Only one of these weapons has been located. It was produced during the 1920s and is, as its designation indicated, a scaled down Luger having an overall length of $6\frac{1}{4}$in. with a barrel 2.15/16in., and a five round magazine.

·22 Conversion Unit—A number of ·22 conversion units were manufactured all of which are rare. The most common is the neatly boxed Erma conversion which includes the barrel and toggle assembly.

32 Round Magazine—A 32 round drum magazine was issued in two versions with a loading device and also a very rare unloading device. This magazine should be treated with care as it contains an extremely powerful spring which can, if not handled correctly, cause considerable damage.
A number of shoulder stocks were issued, the most common of which is the flat board type. This was

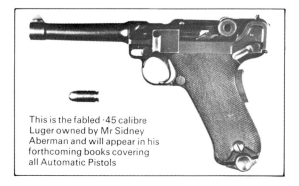

This is the fabled ·45 calibre Luger owned by Mr Sidney Aberman and will appear in his forthcoming books covering all Automatic Pistols

often issued in conjunction with the above magazine, forming an effective collapsible carbine. As with most weapons there were a number of different types of cleaning rods issued and also a stripping tool. This stripping tool is interesting as it doubles as a loading device for the standard magazine. The long discussed resumption of production of the Luger by Mauser has at last been confirmed and production has now begun again—proof of the greatness of Hugo Borchardt's concept and of George Luger's refinement of the design.

Type	Barrel	Calibre
Borchardt, Loewe or DWM with shoulder stock	7 3/8"	7·65
1900 American Eagle	4 3/4"	7·65
1900 American Eagle	4 3/4"	7·65
1900 Bulgarian	4 3/4"	7·65
1900 Portuguese Commercial	4 3/4"	7·65
1900 Commercial	4 3/4"	7·65
1900 Swiss Commercial	4 3/4"	7·65
1900 Swiss Military	4 3/4"	7·65
1902 Commercial GL	4 3/4"	7·65
1902 Carbine Experimental	11 7/8"	7·65
1902 Carbine	11 7/8"	7·65
1902 Commercial	4"	9mm
1902 American Eagle	4"	9mm
1902 Cartridge Counter	4"	9mm
1902 Presentation Carbine	11 7/8"	7·65
1902 Stoeger Carbine	11 7/8"	7·65
1902 Presentation	7"	7·65
1902 ProtoCommercial	4"	7·65
1903 Proto Commercial	4"	7·65
1903 Transition	4"	7·65
GL Baby Luger	3"	9mm
1904 Navy	6"	9mm
1904/06 Prototype	Varies 4-7'	7·65/9mm
1906 U.S. Test	5"	·45 ACP
1906 French Commercial	4 3/4"	7·65
1906 Russian	4"	9mm
1906 Portuguese Navy	4"	9mm
1906 Bulgarian	4"	9mm
1906 Portuguese Army	4 3/4"	7·65
1906 Portuguese Army	4"	9mm
1906 Swiss Military	4 3/4"	7·65
1906 Swiss Police	4 3/4"	7·65
1906 American Eagle	4 3/4"	7·65
1906 American Eagle	4"	9mm
1906 Commercial	4"	9mm
1906 Commercial	4 3/4"	7·65
1906 Navy Commercial	6"	9mm
1906 Navy Military	6"	9mm
1907 Navy Military	6"	9mm
1906/07 Brazilian	4 3/4"	7·65
1908 Commercial	4"	9mm
1908 Navy Commercial	6"	9mm/7·65
1908 Portuguese	4"	9mm
1908 Bulgarian	4"	9mm
1908 Navy Military	6"	9mm
1908 Military	4"	9mm
1908 3rd Issue Military	4"	9mm
1913 DWM Commercial	4"	9mm
1914 DWM Commercial	4"	9mm
1914 DWM Military	4"	9mm
1914 Erfurt Military	4"	9mm
1914 Erfurt Artillery	8"	9mm
1914 DWM Artillery	8"	9mm
1914 DWM Navy	6"	9mm
1918 Spandau	4"	9mm
1920 Double-date Artillery	8"	9mm
1920 Dated Navy	4"	9mm
Double-Dated Military	4"	9mm
1920 Commercial	3 5/8" & 4"	9mm/7·65
1920 Commercial	3 7/8"	7·65
1920 Simson	4"	9mm
1920 Swiss	4" & 4 3/4"	7·65
1920 Carbine	11 7/8"	7·65
1920 Abercombie & Fitch	4 3/4"	9mm/7·65
1920 Stoegers	3 5/8" & 8"	9mm/7·65
1920 Navy	6"	9mm
1920/22 Dated	4"	9mm/7·65
'Death Head' (1917-18)	4"	9mm
Arabic Police	4"	9mm
1920 Kireghoff	3 7/8"	7·65
1920 Side Frame HK	3 7/8"	7·65
1923 Commercial	3 7/8"	7·65
1923 Safe/Loaded	3 7/8"	7·65
1923 Navy	6"	9mm
1923 Russian	3 7/8"	7·65
1923 Simson	4"	9mm
1923 Simson Commercial	4"	7·65
1925/26/27 Simson	8"	9mm
1924 Swiss Bern	4 3/4"	7·65
1929 Persian Artillery	8"	9mm
1929 Swiss Bern	4 3/4"	7·65
1933 Stoeger	4" & 8"	9mm/7·65
1939 Finnish Navy	4"	9mm
'06 Dutch	4"	7·65
1923 Dutch	4"	9mm
Vickers	4"	9mm
Vickers Commercial	4"	9mm
1933 Dutch	4"	9mm
1937/40 Dutch, Mauser	4"	9mm
1929/33 Riff	4"	9mm
1933 'Sneak'	4"	9mm
1933 SD-1, 2, 3, 4, 5, 6	4"	9mm
1933 KI	4"	9mm
Oberndorf	4" & 4 3/4"	9mm
Oberndorf Commercial	4"	9mm/7·65
K-date	4"	9mm
K-date Marine	4"	9mm
Oberndorf Toggle	4"	9mm
G-date DWM	4"	9mm
G-date S/42	4"	9mm
S/42 1936-39	4"	9mm
42 1939-40	4"	9mm
S/42 Navy	4"	9mm
Cutaways	4"	9mm
Engraved Lugers	4" & 8"	9mm
41 and 42 BYF (Mauser)	4"	9mm
BYF Black Widow	4"	9mm
SS Marked	4"	9mm
H. Krieghoff Sideframe	4"	9mm
H. Krieghoff Sideframe	4"	7·65
P-Code Commercial HK	4"	9mm
S-Code HK	4"	9mm
36 Dated HK	4"	9mm
1936-37 HK	4"	9mm
1938-39 HK	4"	9mm
1940 HK	4"	9mm
1941 HK	4"	9mm
1942-44 HK	4"	9mm
1945 HK	4"	9mm
1945 Commercial	4"	9mm
KU Marked (BYF and 42/41)	4"	9mm
1940 BYF Krieghoff	4"	9mm
UB Test Mauser	4"	9mm
41/42 Mauser	4"	9mm
1940 Jap, 42 Toggle	4"	9mm
S-Toggle Simson	4"	9mm
1935 Persian	4"	9mm
'GNR' Mauser Banner	4 3/4"	7·65
Banner Commercial	4"	9mm
Swiss Banner dated 1937	4 3/4"	7·65
Latvian Banner	4 3/4"	7·65
Latvian Banner	4"	9mm
Austrian Banner	4"	9mm
1936-39 Banners	4"	9mm
1940-42 Banners	4"	9mm
1940-41 Banners	4"	9mm
1940-42 Banners	4"	9mm

Thanks must be given to Ralph Shattuck who has given his permission to use photographs of his magnificent collection of Lugers and also the table of Lugers produced.

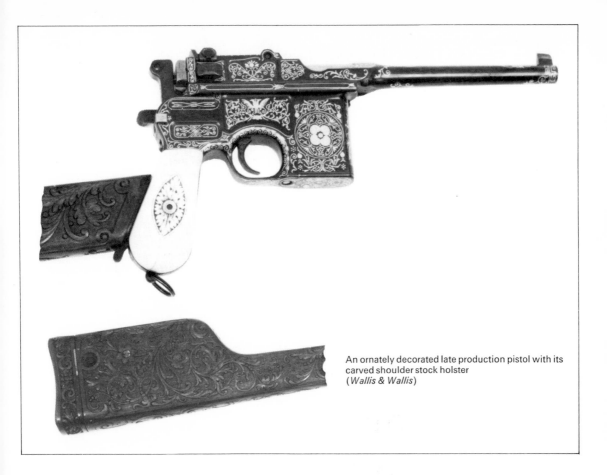

An ornately decorated late production pistol with its
carved shoulder stock holster
(*Wallis & Wallis*)

The Mauser 1896

by A. J. R. Cormack

Peter Paul Mauser was born on 24 June 1838, one
of fourteen children. His father was a master
gunsmith with the Government Firearms Factory
in Oberndorf. The town of Oberndorf which became
famous as the home of the Mauser factory is on the
river Neckar. At the age of fourteen, in 1852,
Paul and his brother Wilhelm joined their father at
the factory. Owing to the lack of demand for
military weapons the Government Firearms Factory
was closed and Peter and Wilhelm were made
redundant and paid off. During this period of
unemployment Paul Mauser designed and sold
manufacturing licences of his famous Mauser
Model 71 rifle. With the money thus obtained Paul
and Wilhelm decided to set up a Firearms business
in a small factory in Oberndorf. Their intention was
to produce the Model 71 rifle themselves. This
was very successful as with the continued sales
of the weapon they even managed to build a new
factory. The State, deciding that although there
was no immediate need for weapons, thought it
would be prudent to secure a supplier, if and when
the need should arise. They therefore offered the

Mauser brothers the opportunity to purchase the
old Government Firearms Factory. With this offer
went the promise of financial help in the form of a
bank loan. The brothers accepted and the firm was
named Mauser Brothers & Company. Eight years
later, in 1882, Wilhelm died leaving Paul in complete
control of the factory. The name of the firm was
changed in 1884 to Waffenfabrik Mauser.
Possibly through lack of capital or maybe from a
desire to return to the pure development of
weapons without the financial worries of their
manufacture, Paul sold a controlling interest in
Waffenfabrik Mauser to Ludwick Loewe & Company
in 1887.
Paul Mauser retained a position in the firm
which gave full freedom to his interest in the
design and development of weapons. He was put
in charge of that department of the factory. During
the period 1893 to 1894 the Mauser pistol known
as the Model 1896 or Model '96 was designed.
The Mauser firm came under the control of
Deutsche Waffen and Munition Fabriken. This firm,
known by its initials DWM was formed by the

amalgamation of Ludwig Loewe and the German Metallic Cartridge Company in 1896.

There are two distinct schools of thought as to the designer of the Model 1896. The first is that the pistol was designed by Fidel Feederle and his brothers who were members of the Mauser Design Department and that at a later stage Mauser himself took over responsibility of the production and tidying up of the pistol. The second school believes that Mauser himself designed the pistol. It is probable that either a combination of, or both of these theories could be correct as in the design or development of a weapon or component it is often shared amongst the staff. As Paul Mauser was the head of the department it is definite that he and the Feederle brothers would all be intimately concerned with whatever work was being carried out. One thing that is certain is that the patents which were taken out were signed by Paul Mauser as the designer of the pistol. In 1910 the first of the pocket pistols came out of the Mauser Factory. Production of the later HSC was to be resumed after the Second World War, thus continuing the long tradition of the manufacture of pocket pistols. On 29 May 1914 Paul Mauser died. It is perhaps fortunate that he did not live to see the death and destruction caused by the weapons produced in what had once been his factory. During the years after Mauser's death a number of pistols were designed and produced by the Mauser factory including the WTP and the aforementioned HSC. After the Second World War the complete Mauser Plant was razed to the ground and it was not until 1964 that Mauser resumed the production of pistols.

Model 1896

The Model 1896 was first patented on 11 December 1895. One Mauser photograph shows an early pistol with the date 15 March 1895 ; this date is probably that of the trial rather than the design. Apart from the use of a spur hammer and the chambering of the pistol for the Borchardt cartridge there is very little difference between this pistol and any of the later pistols. The major mechanical difference, one shared with the first production pistols, was the use of a single locking lug on the bolt. This proved satisfactory with the lower-powered Borchardt cartridge but proved insufficient when the increased power of the true Mauser round was developed. As all models of the 1896 produced after the first production batch are very similar externally and internally, a number of features have been chosen to aid identification of the various models. The serial number ranges applied to their production of the model of 1896 are unfortunately of little help as not only do the features overlap in serial sequence, but presumably in an attempt to impress potential customers with their sales volume, Mauser missed large blocks of numbers. In many cases these missing blocks were never used and so precise serial number details are impossible to obtain. The basic division of the identification features are : side panel milling patterns ; firing pin ; extractor ; safety catch ; trigger and hammer variations. Some

of these features are so distinctive to the block of pistols in which they are incorporated that they have given their name to the group. To give a clear understanding of these features so that an individual pistol can be identified with the text each feature will be described in detail.

Frame Milling

There are four basic types of frame milling. The first has both the sides of the frame milled with the same pattern ; the second type—the later cone hammer pistols and some of the first large ring pistols had a different pattern for the left side to that used on the first type. This is in the shape of a square inside the square frame of the earlier type. The flat side where there are no milling cut-outs at all. The final type, of which there are minor variations, has the same left side square cut out as the second type but has the right side milled in a different pattern of cuts outs. Reference to the diagram will show the precise patterns. The Schnellfeuer has an individual frame pattern that does not fit into any of these groups.

Firing Pins

The first type of firing pin is retained in the same manner as the Colt 1911 A1 i.e. by the use of a vertically sliding block. The second and third types are both removed by pushing in and turning through 90° and pulling out rearward. The difference between the two is that the early type has one retaining lug and the second type two.

Extractor

There are only two types of extractor. The early type is narrower and parallel sided while the later type is wider and has protrusions just behind the claw.

Trigger

Of the two types of trigger, the first has the trigger itself pivoted on a block that is pinned to the frame and the second type pivots directly in the frame.

Safety Catch

There are four types of safety, the first of which is operated by moving the lever down for safe. The second type is applied by moving the lever upwards. The third type, the New Safety (Neue Sicherung) or NS can only be applied when the hammer is cocked and pulled back slightly. The last type enables the hammer to be dropped when the safety is applied.

Hammer

The three basic types of hammer are the cone, so named because of the multiple concentric layers of metal rising to a cone on each side. The second type, the large ring type is so named because of the large hole in the hammer. The last, the small ring, has a small hole in the hammer.

These above identification features can in combination enable most models of the Mauser 1896 to be identified, however as with many weapons that have been continually developed, there is a considerable overlap of features.

Frame

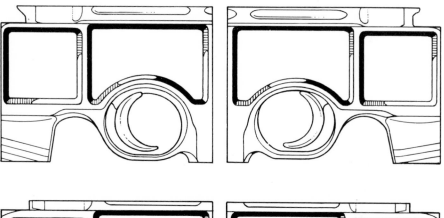

First type

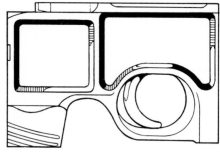 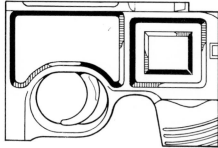

Second type

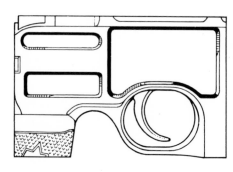 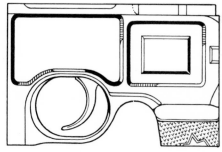

Third type

Right   *Left*

Extractor

Early type

Late type

Firing Pin

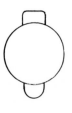

Late

Two lug

Early

One lug

The Step Barrel Model

This model, the first production version of the 1896, takes its name from the step or difference in diameter of the barrel which occurs before the frame. It features a single locking lug on the bolt and is the only production version of the pistol to have this feature. It has a cone hammer and all the early features, earliest frame milling, firing pin, extractor, trigger and safety catch. The pistol is chambered for the 7·63 Mauser cartridge and can have a six, ten or a twenty shot magazine loaded through the top of the frame by stripper clip. The barrel is 5¼in long. The production period of the Step Barrelled pistols was of a relatively short duration, there being only just over 200 manufactured.

The Cone Hammer Model

The barrel step of the earlier pistol was replaced on the Cone Hammer by a more streamlined shape. The firing pin, safety, trigger and extractor are of the earliest type. The frame milling on the earliest pistols was of the first type but this was superseded by the second type early in production. The hammer, from which the model takes its name is the cone type. The barrel extension is strengthened with lighter milling cuts. The barrel length is 5½in and the pistol was sold in six, ten or twenty shot versions, the twenty shot version being extremely rare. A contract for 1000 pistols was obtained from Turkey

and a reasonable number of pistols were sold on the commercial market.

A variation of the standard pistol is one fitted with a 4½in barrel and fixed sights. This was manufactured in either six or ten shot versions. Many models of the Cone Hammer type were supplied to the English gun trade. The standard Cone Hammer had a ten shot magazine. Most variants including the twenty shot magazine were available with the shoulder stock holster.

Large Ring Hammer

A number of transitional weapons were produced with the early features and the second type of frame milling. These pistols led to the purchase by the Italian government of more than five thousand of the Model 1896.

The Italian designation was 'Pistole Automatiche Modello-1899'. This Italian contract has a flat-sided frame, a 5½in barrel and a ten round magazine. The safety and extractor are of the early type, the trigger the late type and the firing pin the one-lug type. After the Italian contract a standard production pistol was produced identical to the contract weapons except for the frame milling which was of the second pattern. A variation of the large ring hammer type is the six shot. This pistol has the late two-lug firing pin unlike the earlier weapon.

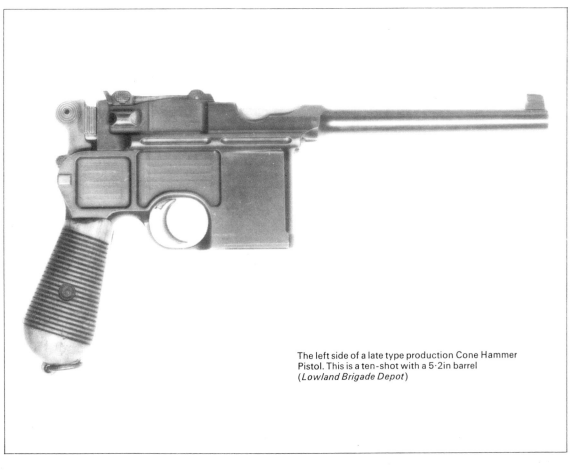

The left side of a late type production Cone Hammer Pistol. This is a ten-shot with a 5·2in barrel (*Lowland Brigade Depot*)

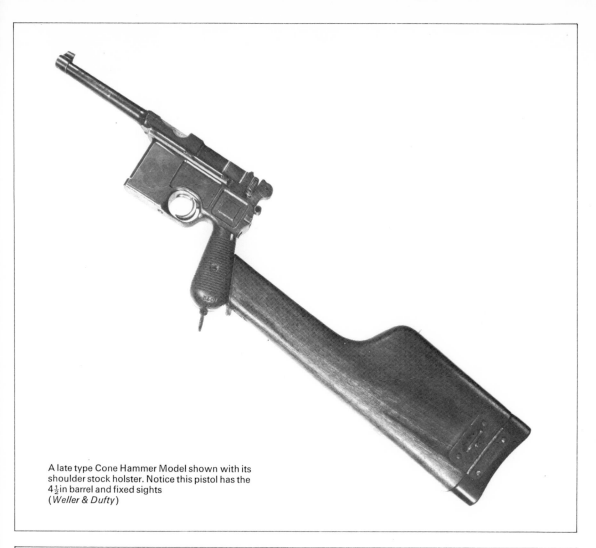

A late type Cone Hammer Model shown with its
shoulder stock holster. Notice this pistol has the
4½in barrel and fixed sights
(*Weller & Dufty*)

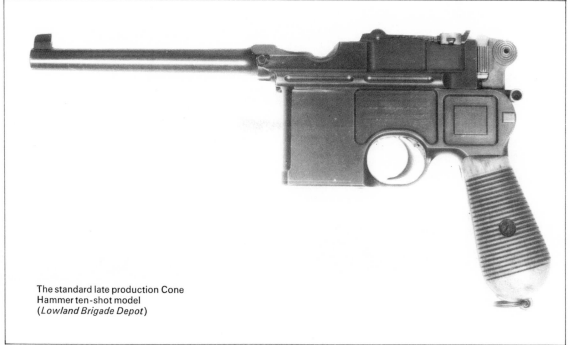

The standard late production Cone
Hammer ten-shot model
(*Lowland Brigade Depot*)

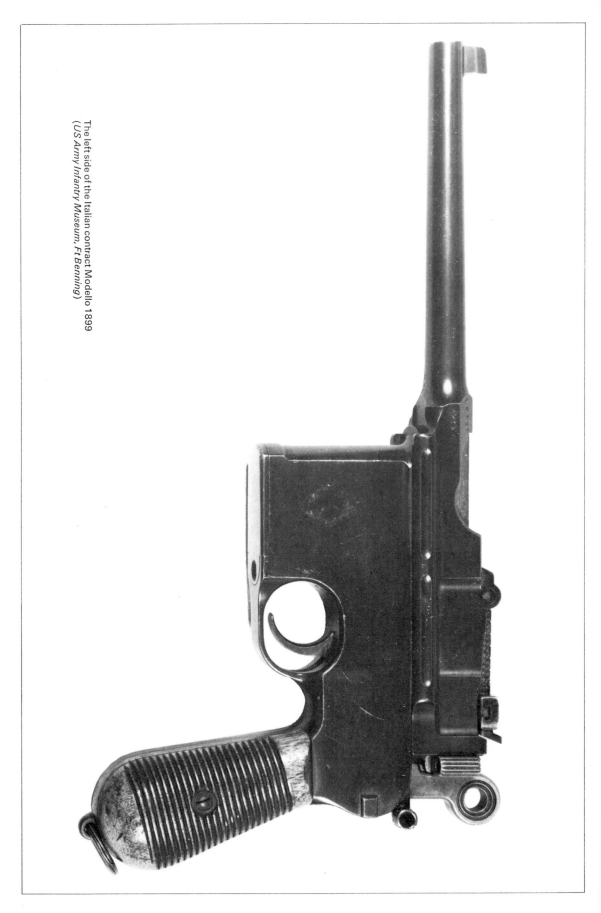

The left side of the Italian contract Modello 1899
(*US Army Infantry Museum, Ft Benning*)

A flat side Large Ring Hammer Pistol of the Italian Contract type
(*US Army Infantry Museum, Ft Benning*)

The left side of the Large Ring Hammer Pistol showing the frame milling
(*US Army Infantry Museum, Ft Benning*)

A standard production Large Ring Hammer Pistol
(*US Army Infantry Museum, Ft Benning*)

Pre-war Standard Production Type

This is the production pattern standardised before the First World War. The pistol has a 5½in barrel and a ten shot magazine, and all the late features other than the safety which is of the second type. During production the rifling was changed from four to six grooves. This is probably the most commonly found version of the Model 1896.

A variation on the standard was the chambering of a small number of pistols for the straight sided

Mauser Export 9mm Cartridge. The difference between the 9mm Parabellum, the 9mm Export and the 7·63 Mauser are as follows:

	9mm Mauser Export	9mm Parabellum	7·63 Mauser
Case length	·976 – ·988	·740 – ·756	·944 – 1·044
Case neck diam.	·376 – ·380	·374 – ·481	·319 – ·314
Case rim diam.	·387 – ·393	·386 – ·393	·388 – ·393
Bullet weight	125 gr	125 gr	85–90 gr
Velocity	1360 fps	1130 fps	1453 fps

Standard pre-war production type 1896

Right side of frame showing the Mauser name and the Small Ring Hammer (*Author's Collection*)

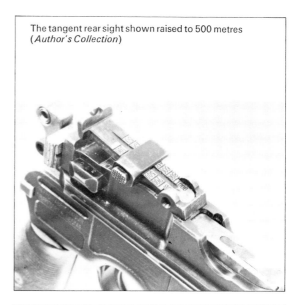

The tangent rear sight shown raised to 500 metres (*Author's Collection*)

The Hammer shown in the down position with the safety catch off
Author's Collection

The Hammer shown raised with the safety catch applied
Author's Collection

The 9mm Mauser Export is the most powerful 9mm cartridge to be used as standard in any pistol.
It also had a very limited use in a SIG submachine gun.
Other than the calibre and the resultant milling on the top of the magazine follower to accommodate the straight walled cartridge the pistol has no major changes.
A contract for the Persian government has a

Persian Crest on the left of the frame and is based on the standard pistol. The collector must beware of any Persian contract pistol that is offered, as the pistol being almost identical to the standard pistol is easily faked.
One indication of the authenticity of the pistol is the border on the left side of the frame round the crest. On the true contract weapon this is narrower than that on the standard pistol.

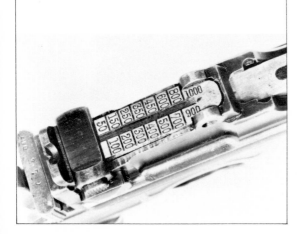

The markings on the tangent rear sight. These are in metres
(*Author's Collection*)

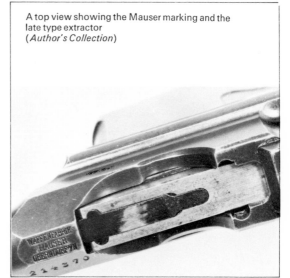

A top view showing the Mauser marking and the late type extractor
(*Author's Collection*)

The Bolt shown to the rear. Notice the locking lugs
Author's Collection

A clip of cartridges shown being loaded into the Mauser 1896
Author's Collection

The right side of the 1916 Contract 9mm Pistol.
Notice the '9' burnt into the grip
(*Bowman*)

A German Contract 9mm Parabellum Model 1896
(*Bowman*)

Wartime Production Commercial (W.W.I.)

The wartime commercial varies from previous pistols in that it is the first model to incorporate the New Safety. This is indicated by the letters NS on the back of the hammer. A variation on the War Time Commercial was the German government contract which was lodged in 1916 although not all of the contract was manufactured by the end of the war. Because of the desire of the German army to standardise on one calibre, the 9mm Parabellum, the pistol was manufactured in this calibre. Outwardly the finish is poor and to differentiate from the 7·63 version a large 9 (sometimes filled with red paint) is burned into the grips.

Post War Variants

After the war a number of alterations were made to the standard variations already produced. These included weapons either modified or manufactured to comply with the Treaty of Versailles. The modifications consisted of a shortened barrel usually under 4in and the removing of the adjustable sight. A number of oddities have turned up such as the use of the Bolo Small Frame with long barrels, the standard frame with Bolo barrel, pistols with Luger front sights and even pistols rebarrelled with Luger barrels. These variations are the inevitable result of the continuous production of the pistol.

The Post War Commercial Model (W.W.I.)

The production of the Post War Commercial pistol as opposed to the previously mentioned Versailles pistol featured a 5½in barrel and the last type of safety. All the other features are of the latest type. The barrel has a shallow step in it further forward on the barrel than that of the early Step Barrel weapon. The panel to the rear of the left side has a Mauser banner trade mark engraved on it.

Bolo Models

The Bolo name possibly comes from the use of the pistol by the Bolsheviks. The smaller frame and shorter barrel are easily recognised in comparison with the standard pistol. The first of the small frame Bolo models is of the Large Ring Hammer Type and has a barrel length of 3·9in and a ten round magazine. The features are the same as the standard production Large Ring Hammer but as with the six shot the firing pin is of the two lug type. The Bolo pistol continued with a Small Hammer version. This has a 3·8in barrel, a late type trigger and two lug firing pin, and the second safety that works in the upward direction. The extractor is however of the early type. The frame milling is of the late type. The next Bolo model has a late trigger, extractor and a two lug firing pin with the second type safety. After the end of the First World War Bolo production was resumed with all the late type features and either the New Safety (NS) or the last type. Other than reworked variants these of the post war period were the last of the Small Frame Bolo pistols produced.

Schnellfeuer

The Schnellfeuer was developed to combat the

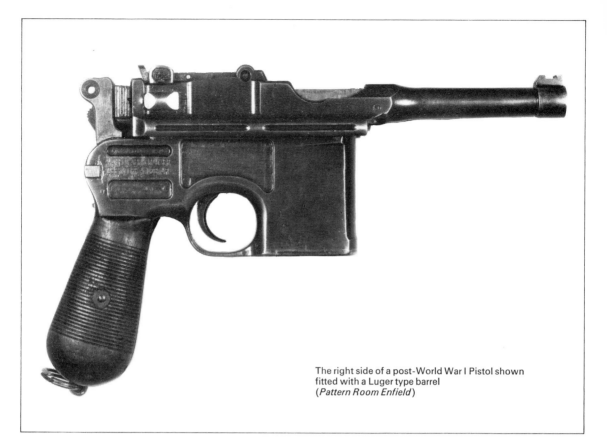

The right side of a post-World War I Pistol shown
fitted with a Luger type barrel
(*Pattern Room Enfield*)

A late type post-war Commerical.
Notice the lack of milling on the rail below the barrel extension
compared to that of the early type
(*Pattern Room, Enfield*)

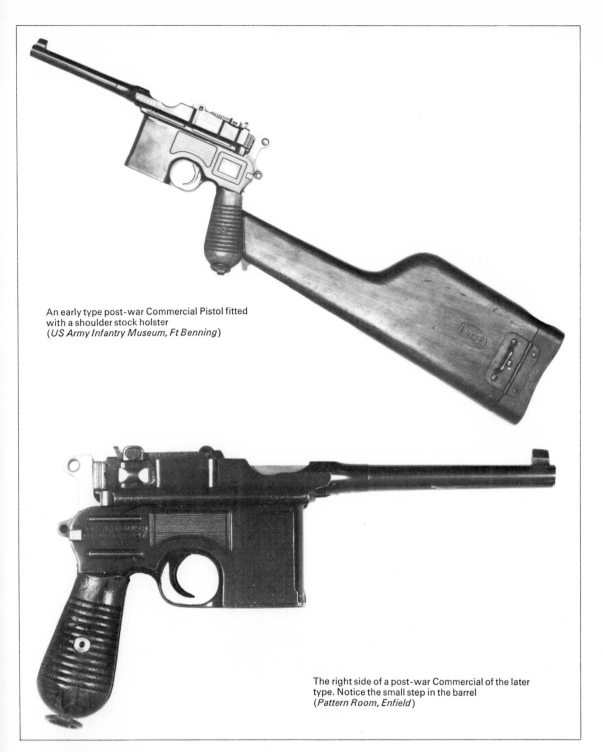

An early type post-war Commercial Pistol fitted
with a shoulder stock holster
(*US Army Infantry Museum, Ft Benning*)

The right side of a post-war Commercial of the later
type. Notice the small step in the barrel
(*Pattern Room, Enfield*)

increasing number of sales of the rapid fire Spanish
pistols that were outwardly copies of the Mauser
but featured fully automatic fire. Such a pistol is the
Astra (See Profile No 15).

There were two separate patents taken out for
versions of the Schnellfeuer, one the Nickl and
the other the Westinger. Both were assigned to
the Mauser Company. They differ in the method
of achieving the selective fire and externally
in the shape of the switch. The Westinger has
a squashed diamond shape with a pointed top.

The pistols incorporated all the latest type
features but have different triggers and selector
switches. The magazine is detachable and
can be either ten or twenty shots, however,
the pistol can still be loaded from the top by a
stripper clip. The effect of these pistols is, owing to
the uncontrollable muzzle climb, more theoretical
than practical. (A typical submachine gun, the
Sterling, which is heavier and more easily held,
rises at a rate of 40° per second during which
time only 8 rounds are fired).

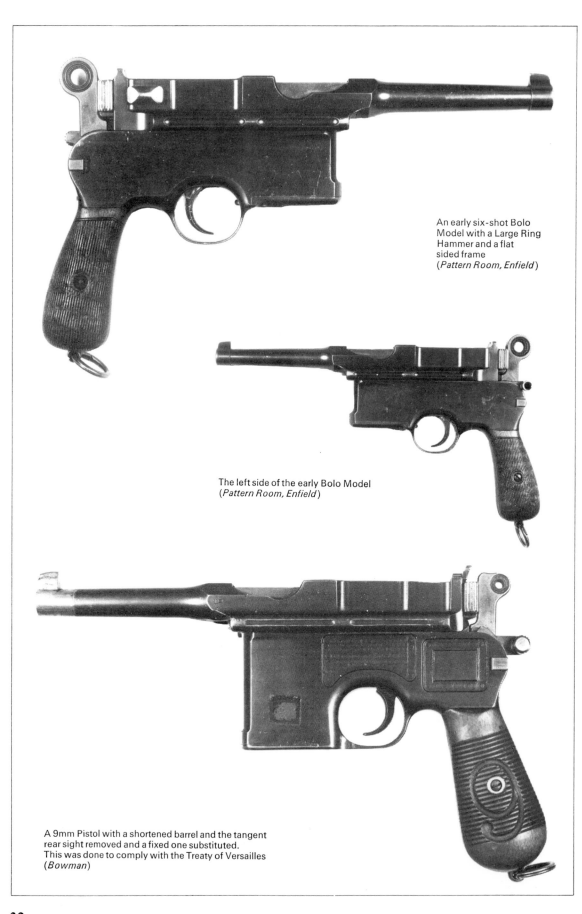

An early six-shot Bolo
Model with a Large Ring
Hammer and a flat
sided frame
(*Pattern Room, Enfield*)

The left side of the early Bolo Model
(*Pattern Room, Enfield*)

A 9mm Pistol with a shortened barrel and the tangent
rear sight removed and a fixed one substituted.
This was done to comply with the Treaty of Versailles
(*Bowman*)

A Presentation Bolo Pistol of the post-war type
(*R. Dalgleish*)

A post-war ten-shot Bolo fitted with the tangent sight
(*Pattern Room, Enfield*)

The left side of the Schnellfeuer with a ten-round magazine
(*US Army Infantry Museum, Ft Benning*)

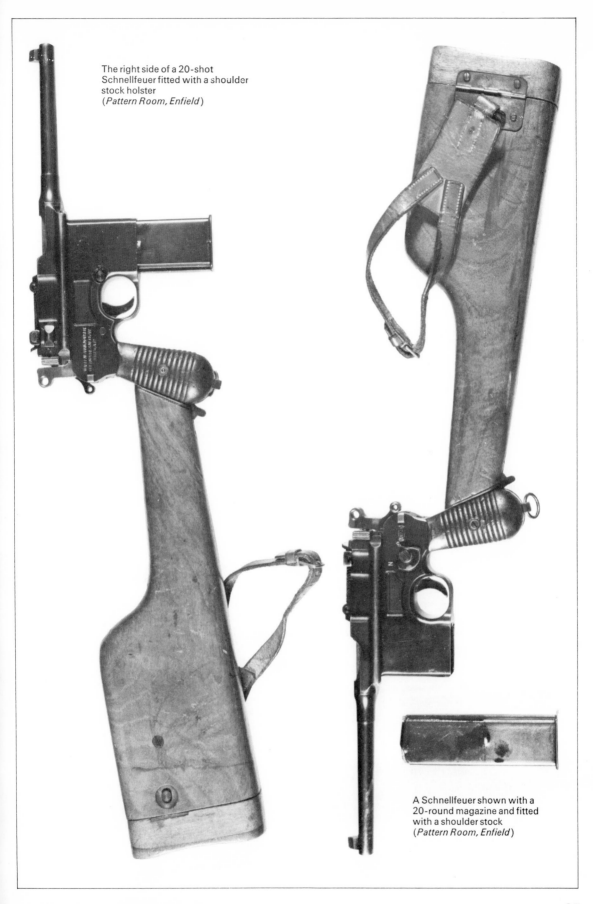

The right side of a 20-shot
Schnellfeuer fitted with a shoulder
stock holster
(*Pattern Room, Enfield*)

A Schnellfeuer shown with a
20-round magazine and fitted
with a shoulder stock
(*Pattern Room, Enfield*)

Mauser Carbine

The Carbine was produced in prototype form in 1897 and in small numbers until the W.W.I. As a result the features vary as with the standard pistol. After the War an attempt was made to redesign the carbine with a removable magazine but this was not pursued. Small, Large and Cone hammers are found as are both types of trigger and extractor. The safety is usually of the first two types. The Mauser was copied by the Spanish, as has been mentioned, but there are also Chinese copies. These are explained by the large number of Mauser 1896 pistols sold to the Chinese and the resultant desire to home-produce. There is usually no difficulty in deciding whether the pistol is of Mauser manufacture as both the Spanish and Chinese have either poor finish, incorrect markings or the internal mechanism varies.

It must be noted that unlike some of its illustrious competitors such as the Colt and Luger, the Model 1896 never achieved vast military sales. Extensive tests were held by numerous European governments. In addition the United States carried out a comprehensive test in 1899 and 1900. It was indeed unfortunate that there was no great military sale as a result of these tests. It is, therefore, true to say that the Mauser may not have been a military success but with its great number of sales on the commercial market it must be considered at least as successful in this field as some of its rivals. Nearly half of the total production between 1897 and 1905 when a total of 46,500 was manufactured was commercial. This high number of COMMERCIALLY sold weapons was the result of the Russian, British and other armies allowing their officers to purchase their side arms personally and many chose the Mauser. The reason was a reliable pistol, available off the shelf.

A military success the 1896 may not have been with its odd shape and difficult and precise construction, but whenever a war has been fought, until the end of the Second World War, the Mauser was at the front. What was the pistol which Sir Winston Churchill chose ? The 1896 naturally. Today the pistol remains as one of the reminders of an age when the stamping and pressing were unknown and the craftsman reigned supreme.

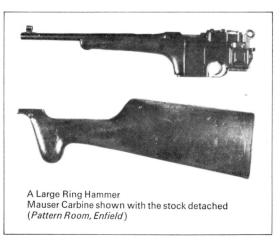

A Large Ring Hammer Mauser Carbine shown with the stock detached (*Pattern Room, Enfield*)

The Large Ring Hammer Mauser Carbine (*Pattern Room, Enfield*)

Walther PP 7·65mm presented to U.S.
General Manton S. Eddy
(*U.S. Army Infantry Museum, Ft. Benning*)

Shown left: Right side of presentation
pistol

Walther Automatic Pistols and Flare Pistols

A. J. R. Cormack

As far back as 1592 gunsmiths from the Thuringia Forest in Germany formed a guild. A centre was established at Zella and its twin town Mehlis. In 1886, three centuries later, Carl Walther at the age of 26 came to Zella to open a gunshop. From this gunshop came the Walther Company, world famous for its precise workmanship and fine craftsmanship and especially renowned for its pistols. A clock may still be seen at nearby Kassel which, although over 200 years old must have been a portent of what was to come. The clock is in the form of a statue of the Greek Goddess Pallas Athene but her lance has been replaced by a pistol !

Carl Walther's main interest at first was to provide rifles for the rapidly expanding sport of target shooting and it was these that he manufactured in Zella Mahlis. These rifles were to reach the top in target shooting where they remain to this day. Although Carl tried to build a number of small calibre automatic pistols, the first successful Walther automatic pistol was not developed until after his death ; it was left to his son Fritz to design a 6·35mm/·32 ACP automatic pistol in 1908. This was

at a time when the Belgian 6·35mm pistols were selling extremely well in Germany and the Model 1908 became an instant success.

Model 1, 2 and 3

The early Walther automatics were designed for low power cartridges and were of a blowback type, but because of the destruction of all records little else is known about them. However, all the pistols were given consecutive numbers and are therefore easily identified. The Model 1 has no features which distinguishes it from the common blowback ·25 ACP automatic pistol. The recoil spring is above the trigger guard under the barrel and the slide is cut away to expose the front part of the barrel.

In 1909 the factory Model 2 was announced. This was an attempt to improve the Model 1 by replacing the recoil spring with one which was concentric with the barrel. A removable barrel bush held the concentric recoil spring and also served as a demounting catch. An odd cocking indicator is incorporated in the rear sight, which operated as follows—when the gun has a round in the chamber

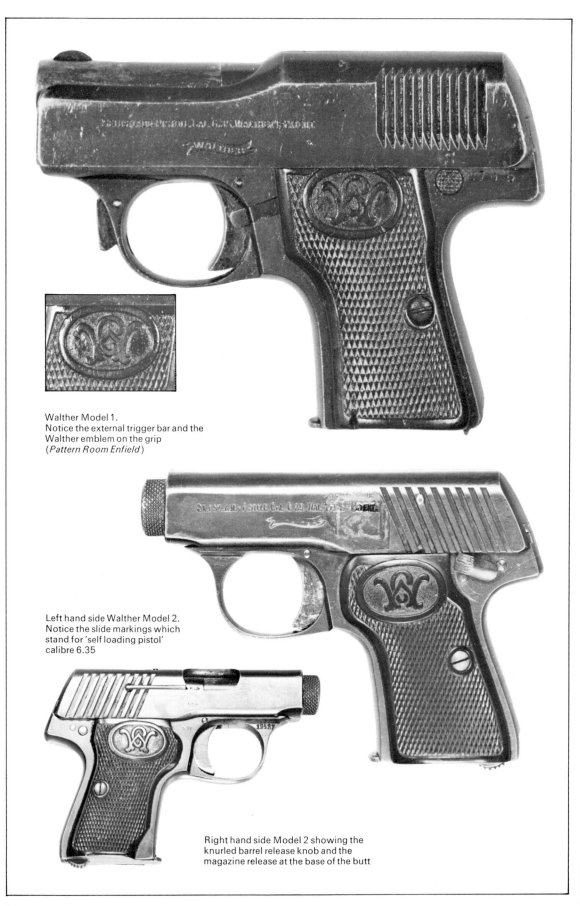

Walther Model 1.
Notice the external trigger bar and the
Walther emblem on the grip
(*Pattern Room Enfield*)

Left hand side Walther Model 2.
Notice the slide markings which
stand for 'self loading pistol'
calibre 6.35

Right hand side Model 2 showing the
knurled barrel release knob and the
magazine release at the base of the butt

Walther model 4—Notice the external trigger bar and different safety lever to the illustration below. The serrations on the rear of the slide also differ

Walther Model 4 calibre 7·65 left side
(*Pattern Room Enfield*)

the sight is in a raised position ready to use, but when the chamber is empty the sight becomes flush with the slide.

The relative success of the Models 1 and 2 resulted in the production of a weapon in a larger calibre than ·25 ACP. This, the Model 3, was outwardly similar to the Model 2 but of heavier construction and chambered for the ·32 ACP cartridge. It was better finished than its predecessors and unusual in that it utilises a left hand ejector port.

Models 4, 5, 6 and 7
With the outbreak of the First World War and the resultant call for weapons the Walther Company produced their Models 4, 5, 6 and 7. The Model 4, a 7·65mm/·32 ACP automatic was once again a logical development of its predecessor with a longer barrel and larger magazine capacity but with the same concentric recoil spring. The slide extension to enable the use of a longer barrel was similar to that used in the Browning Model 22. This weapon saw considerable use in World War I. As there was considerable demand for a well finished pocket pistol, Walther revamped the Model 2 by improving the finish and renamed it the Model 5.

The 9mm parabellum cartridge is normally considered to be too powerful for a blowback designed weapon and weapons chambered for it have some form of locking, or at least a hesitation feature. It is, therefore, strange to realise that the Walther Model 6 was merely an enlarged Model 4 firing the 9mm parabellum round. It must be pointed out that, with these weapons ceasing production in 1917 and possibly having been in considerable use or being subject to wartime production expediencies, their recoil springs or slides may have weakened. Therefore, with the variance in pressures that 9mm parabellum ammunition can develop (from the low power Glisenti 9mm up to the Beretta submachine gun ammunition which may develop pressures in excess of 24,000lb/sq in) it would be the author's recommendation that these weapons be considered collector's items only. If it is contemplated firing them, a most careful check of the mechanical components especially the recoil spring, and the use of one of the lower powered 9mm commercial rounds is recommended.

The Model 7 is merely a smaller version of the Model 6, firing the ·25 ACP cartridge. As it was produced in 1917 when weapons were in short supply it was widely used by German officers.

Models 8 and 9
The mid-20s consolidated the Carl Walther Company with Georg Walther directing the Company's diversifications and Erich Walther the sales, and it was obvious that when the pre-World War II rulers in Germany required small arms they would

Walther Model 4 field stripped
showing clearly the bayonet catch
on the slide extension *Boothroyd*

Right hand side Walther Model 4—
compare the difference in the slide
serrations *(Pattern Room Enfield)*

Compare to illustration left
(Pattern Room Enfield)

Borchardt manufacture by Loewe. Viewed
from left

© *Profile Publications Ltd*

Borchardt viewed from right.
Calibre ·30/7·65mm Borchardt

Luger 1914 Artillery manufactured by D.W.M.
viewed from left.
Actual size—length $12\frac{3}{4}$in, height $5\frac{5}{8}$in, weight
$30\frac{1}{4}$oz, calibre 9mm parabellum

© *Profile Publications Ltd*

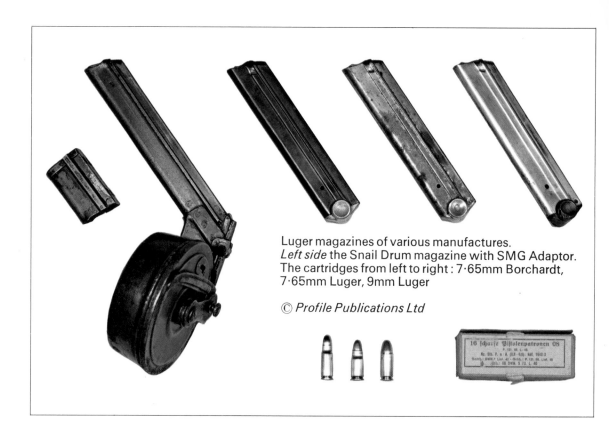

Luger magazines of various manufactures.
Left side the Snail Drum magazine with SMG Adaptor.
The cartridges from left to right : 7·65mm Borchardt,
7·65mm Luger, 9mm Luger

© *Profile Publications Ltd*

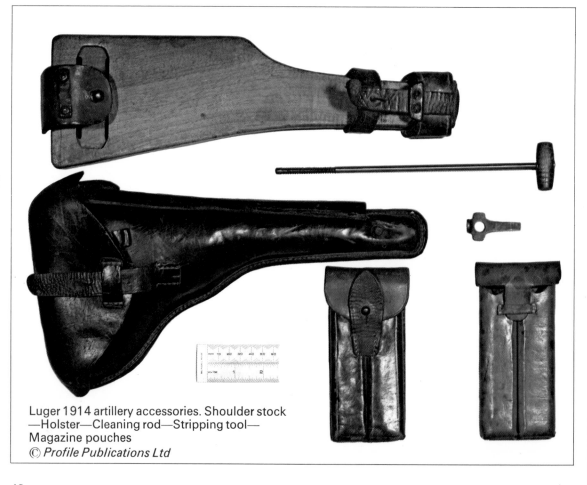

Luger 1914 artillery accessories. Shoulder stock
—Holster—Cleaning rod—Stripping tool—
Magazine pouches
© *Profile Publications Ltd*

Early six-shot flat-side model 1896.
Notice large ring hammer and Bolo grips.

Pattern Room Enfield © *Profile Publications Limited*

Left and right views of a 1896 Mauser
chambered for the 9mm Parabellum cartridge.
Notice the '9' burnt into the grips.

Bowman © *Profile Publications Limited*

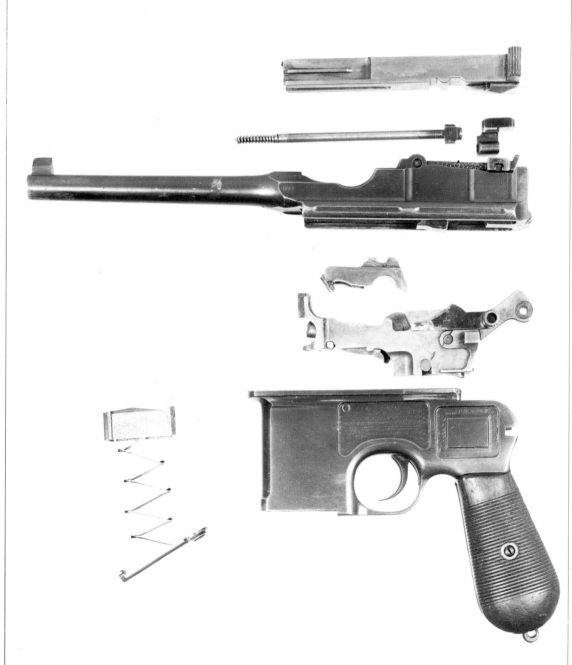

The intricate machine work and interlocking
components are clear when the pistol is
field stripped.

Author's Collection © *Profile Publications Limited*

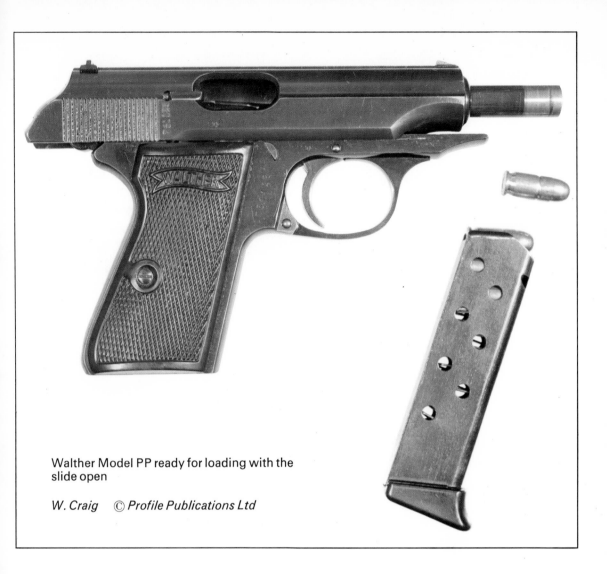

Walther Model PP ready for loading with the slide open

W. Craig   © *Profile Publications Ltd*

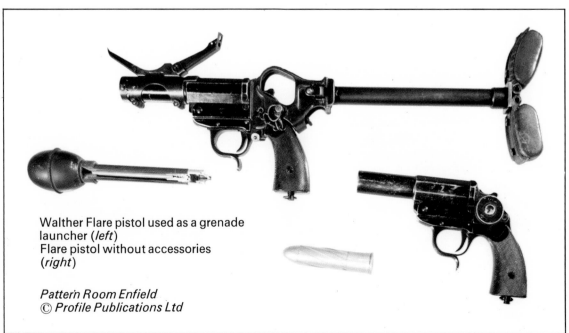

Walther Flare pistol used as a grenade launcher (*left*)
Flare pistol without accessories (*right*)

Pattern Room Enfield
© *Profile Publications Ltd*

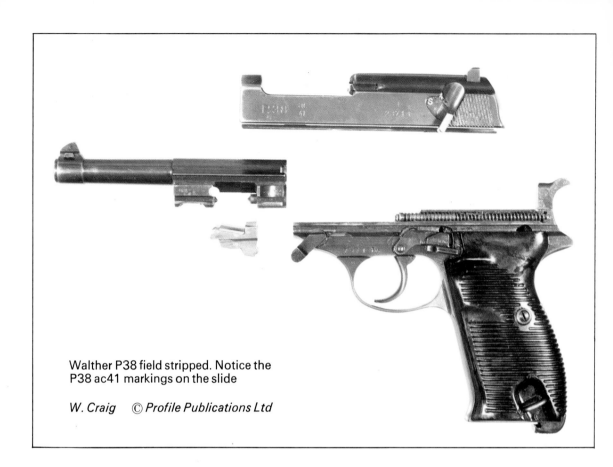

Walther P38 field stripped. Notice the
P38 ac41 markings on the slide

W. Craig © Profile Publications Ltd

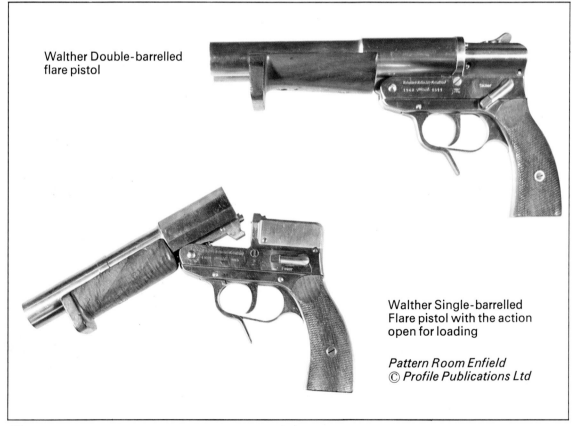

Walther Double-barrelled
flare pistol

Walther Single-barrelled
Flare pistol with the action
open for loading

*Pattern Room Enfield
© Profile Publications Ltd*

U.S. Army issue 1911 A1 of wartime manufacture, notice the relatively poor finish

Bowman © *Profile Publications Limited*

A Colt 1911 A1 manufactured by Union Switch and Signal Company

Bowman © *Profile Publications Limited*

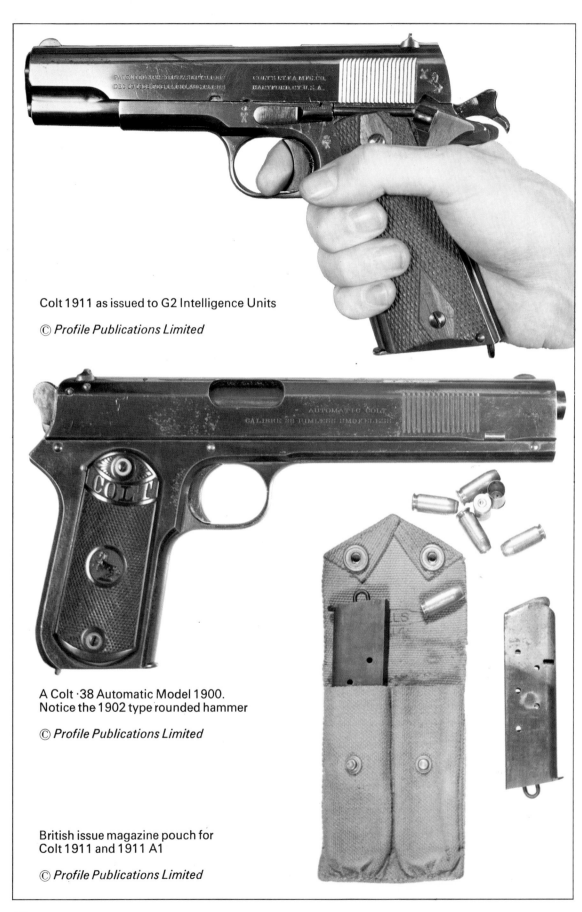

Colt 1911 as issued to G2 Intelligence Units

© *Profile Publications Limited*

A Colt ·38 Automatic Model 1900.
Notice the 1902 type rounded hammer

© *Profile Publications Limited*

British issue magazine pouch for
Colt 1911 and 1911 A1

© *Profile Publications Limited*

Right side of Model 5 showing the serrated barrel nut, injection port and Walther name (*Pattern Room Enfield*)

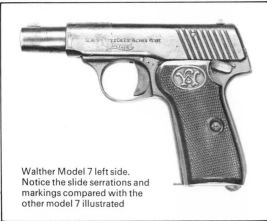

Calibre 6·35 Walther Model 5. Notice the similarity to the Model 2 (*Pattern Room Enfield*)

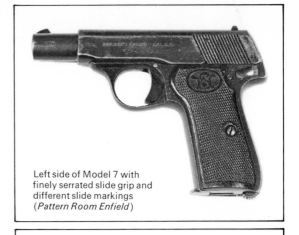

Left side of Model 7 with finely serrated slide grip and different slide markings (*Pattern Room Enfield*)

Right side of Model 7 showing clearly the wide serrations on the slide and the Carl Walther slide markings. Compare these with the fine serrations and different markings below

Walther Model 7 left side. Notice the slide serrations and markings compared with the other model 7 illustrated

turn to the Walther Company. Under the Versailles Treaty Walther had been allowed to manufacture a limited number of small calibre pistols for police use. These included the Models 8 and 9. The Model 8, produced in 1920, in the ·25 calibre was carried by a number of officers during World War II but with such a small calibre it was not an effective combat weapon. However, as a lot of design features of the Model 8 were to reappear in later Walther models it can be considered the forerunner of the modern Walther pistols.

The Model 9 produced in 1921 would seem to have been merely an updated Model 1 and was probably manufactured because of a large market for a weapon with a superior finish. This is confirmed by the large numbers that have been found in either gold or silver finish, some even with engraving. It was sold in limited numbers outside Germany, including a small number to the United States of America.

Models PP and PPK

One of the most famous Walther models was introduced in 1929. This was the Model PP. This pistol was to continue in production throughout the war and is, in fact, still in production. The Model PP is a straight blowback design containing a number of features developed from previous models, in particular the Model 8. The early production weapons were extremely well finished but later weapons produced during the latter part of the war had the signal pin indicator missing and a poor exterior finish.

The Model PP was often issued to German troops owing to the shortage of standard calibre weapons. Although the original calibre was ·32ACP it has also been produced in ·22 Long Rifle and ·380ACP as well as a rare variation in ·25ACP. The designation

49

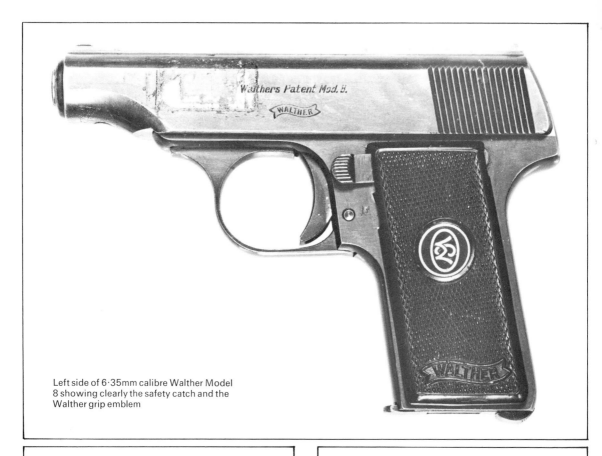

Left side of 6·35mm calibre Walther Model 8 showing clearly the safety catch and the Walther grip emblem

Walther Model 8 right side. Notice the different grip emblem (*Pattern Room Enfield*)

Walther Model 9 left side. Below, the safety catch in the 'on' and 'off' positions

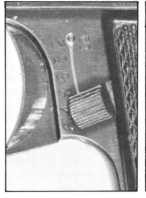 

'PP' is merely derived from the fact that the original use of the pistol was for the police ; thus Polizei Pistole. Some weapons were made with duraluminum receivers with special barrels and, like the Model 9, a great number of presentation finished pistols were manufactured.

It is interesting that the Model PP can be fired in a similar manner to a double action revolver. A steel block allows the weapon to be carried with a round in the chamber and the hammer down in complete safety, and, when needed, the trigger is pulled and the gun fired double action. From the first shot onward the gun works as a normal automatic pistol.

The Walther Model PP 7.65mm top and the Walther
Model PPK 7.65mm bottom *J. Roy*

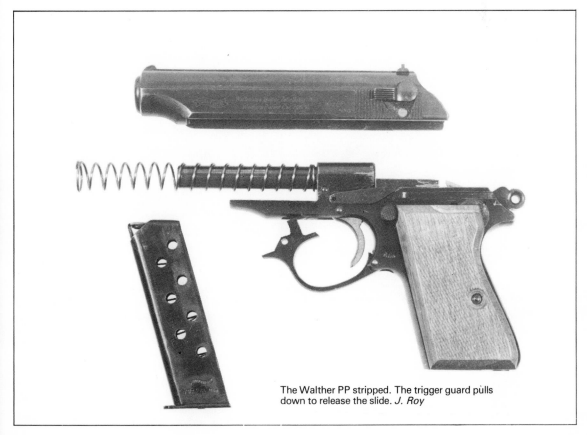

The Walther PP stripped. The trigger guard pulls
down to release the slide. *J. Roy*

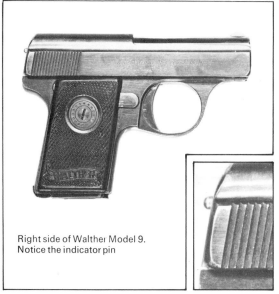

Right side of Walther Model 9.
Notice the indicator pin

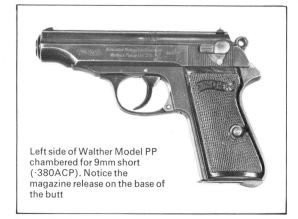

Left side of Walther Model PP
chambered for 9mm short
(·380ACP). Notice the
magazine release on the base of
the butt

Walther PP made under
licence by Manurhin
calibre 9mm   (*Manurhin*)

Walther Model PP chambered
for 7·65mm (·32ACP). Notice
the magazine release on the
frame and the different styles of
magazine bases

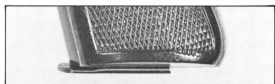

Manurhin manufactured
Walther PP calibre ·22 LR
(*Pattern Room Enfield*)

Right side of licence built
Walther PP

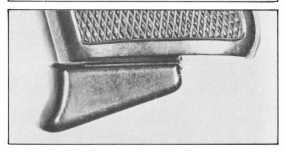

Model PPK

In 1931 a shorter, lighter version of the Model PP
was marketed and as it was originally designed for a
concealed weapon for police and detectives it was
designated the PPK (Polizei Pistole Kriminal).
Physically the gun resembles the Model PP and the
internal mechanics are similar. It saw considerable
use by the German and European police and was
commonly issued, like its larger brother, as a
substitute weapon in the German Army. The weapon
was also manufactured in calibre ·380ACP,
·22 Long Rifle and occasionally in ·25ACP. It must

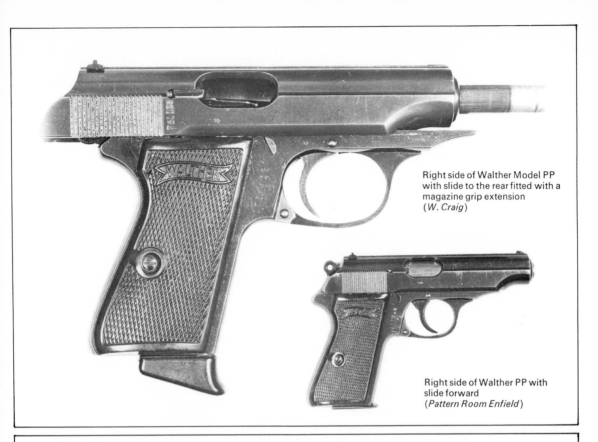

Right side of Walther Model PP with slide to the rear fitted with a magazine grip extension (*W. Craig*)

Right side of Walther PP with slide forward (*Pattern Room Enfield*)

Walther Model PPK. Notice the grip extension fitted to the magazine (*Bowman*)

Walther Model PPK slide detail showing the Nazi acceptance mark also the standard magazine base

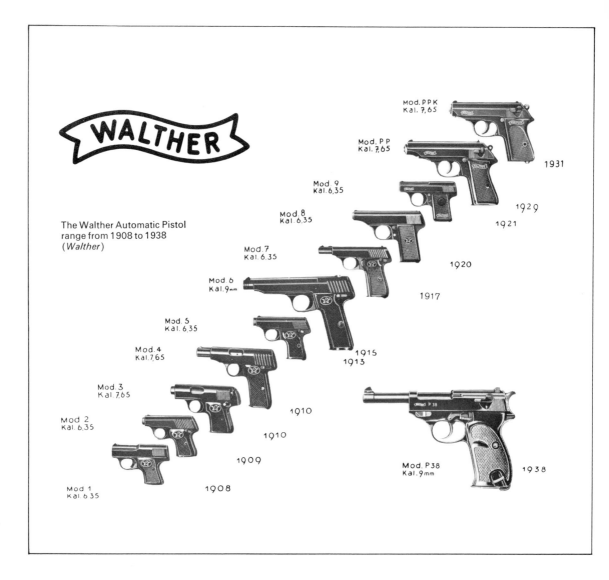

WALTHER

The Walther Automatic Pistol
range from 1908 to 1938
(*Walther*)

Mod. PPK
Kal. 7,65

Mod. PP
Kal. 7,65
1931

Mod. 9
Kal. 6,35
1929

Mod. 8
Kal. 6,35
1921

Mod. 7
Kal. 6,35
1920

Mod. 6
Kal. 9mm
1917

Mod. 5
Kal. 6,35
1915

Mod. 4
Kal. 7,65
1913

Mod. 3
Kal. 7,65
1910

Mod. 2
Kal. 6,35
1910

Mod 1
Kal. 6 35
1908

1909

Mod. P38
Kal. 9mm
1938

be noted that wartime production of both the PP and PPK have some variance in machining, weights, barrel lengths etc. The immortal James Bond carried the Walther PPK

Both the Walther PP and the Walther PPK have been built by a number of firms, either just post-war or at the present time. These include the Turkish Kirikkale which is chambered for ·380ACP or ·32ACP. This weapon is an exact copy of the Walter PP, but manufactured in Turkey. A so-called Mark 2 Version of the PPK is manufactured by Manhurin in calibre ·380ACP. This weapon is identical to the current Walther production PPK. The Manhurin, built under licence after the War, was instrumental in rebuilding Walther, as Walther themselves were banned from production of weapons. The steady flow of royalties from Manhurin enabled the calculating machines to be produced and developed.

An interesting post-war derivation of the PP and PPK is a bastard gun, manufactured to conform to the United States gun control Act of 1968, which dictated the types of gun permitted to be imported. The criteria included a minimum height of 4 inches

and the PPK was only 3·9 inches. Why this minute difference in height should make the gun less useful for nefarious purposes one cannot imagine ! The gun was built by using the PP frame with the PPK slide, barrel and recoil spring. This added about $\frac{1}{8}$ in to the height and thus passed inspection ! The alteration was no doubt carried out as the American market was too lucrative to be ignored. The gun is designated the PPK/s or PPK special.

MP

Under the Treaty of Versailles the Germans were forbidden to produce large calibre pistols and, as can be seen from the Luger 7·65 and Mauser 7·65, which are both easily convertible to 9mm, they made a number of attempts to circumvent this restriction. Walther's contribution to these evasions was the Model MP. The Walther MP would seem to be the least known of Walther productions as it is rumoured that Allied Intelligence had little idea that the pistol was in production before the War, whereas serial numbers would indicate that a considerable number had been manufactured. The design of the MP harks back to the Model 6 as it

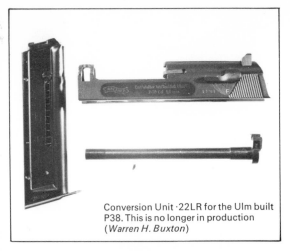

Conversion Unit ·22LR for the Ulm built P38. This is no longer in production (*Warren H. Buxton*)

Early production Model HP. This weapon is fitted with wood grips (*U.S. Army Infantry Museum, Ft. Benning*)

is a blowback pistol firing the 9mm parabellum round. The pistol has a very heavy recoil spring and slide to keep the breech closed during firing. The weapon is identical to the PP in everything but dimensions and even has the double action trigger of that weapon. While a pistol in perfect condition is safe with 9mm parabellum once again it is recommended that the precaution outlined previously should be noted.

HP and P.38

Immediately before the war Walther moved further into the field of 9mm parabellum firearms by the introduction of a Model HP and in 1937 the Heeres Pistole or service pistol was presented to the German officials. Finally in 1938 a modified HP was

Late model HP with plastic grips. This weapon was supplied to the Swedish Infantry (note the stamped number on the slide) under contract (*Warren H. Buxton*)

Right side of Walther HP early type (*U.S. Army Infantry Museum, Ft. Benning*)

Although the hammer is slotted for the indicator pin, this has been omitted on this late war production gun. *J. Roy.*

The PPK showing the indicator pin in the rear of the slide and the slot in the top of the hammer. *J. Roy*

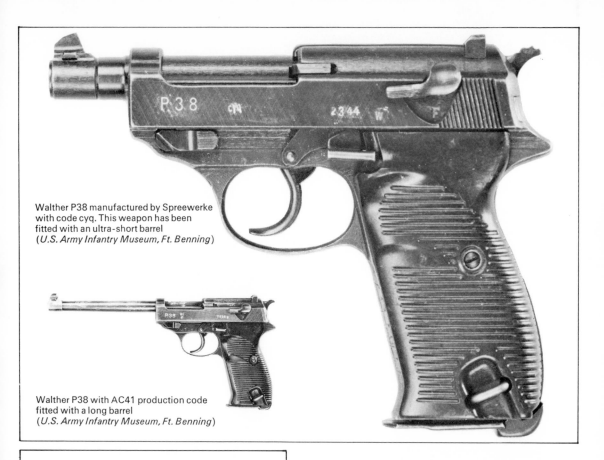

Walther P38 manufactured by Spreewerke with code cyq. This weapon has been fitted with an ultra-short barrel
(*U.S. Army Infantry Museum, Ft. Benning*)

Walther P38 with AC41 production code fitted with a long barrel
(*U.S. Army Infantry Museum, Ft. Benning*)

First German military issue P38 with zero series serial number
(*U.S. Army Infantry Museum, Ft. Denning*)

A P38 with the code 480. This was the first code series used by the Germans
(*Warren H. Buxton*)

adopted by the military staff, along with the Luger, as the standard service side-arm and designated the P38 (pistol Model 1938). Test models of the HP were built in calibre ·38ACP and ·45ACP for the American market and, in fact, a commercial model 9mm HP was marketed by Stoeger Arms of New York in 1939. The finish of the Model HP was always immaculate.

The P38 was adopted by the Army in 1938. The main differences between it and the HP are, apart from the markings on the slide, the checkered wooden grips, the rectangular firing pin and a concealed extractor, making parts non-interchangeable. There were also a number of minor changes made in the P38 during its development.

The first series of Walther P38s during the war had serial numbers beginning with an 0 and the first 1500 of which have the rectangular firing pin of the HP. There would seem to have been three types of markings during development on the basic gun, namely HP, P38 and Model P38. The HP and the Model P38 have German commercial proof marks and are rare. The proof mark was probably used for export or for police units. Also evident, as on other wartime produced German weapons, were the manufacturers' code numbers. The P38 was manufactured by Walther, Mauser and Spreewerk. The codes used on the weapons to conceal the producer's from the allies were as follow: Mauser bfy, svw ; Walther 480, ac ; and Spreewerk cyq. As previously mentioned there were a number of Walthers built which do not come into the general

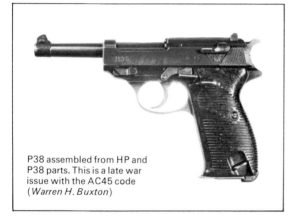

P38 assembled from HP and P38 parts. This is a late war issue with the AC45 code (*Warren H. Buxton*)

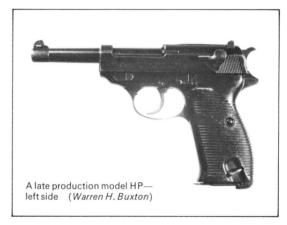

A late production model HP— left side (*Warren H. Buxton*)

production runs. One of these guns was not even assembled ! This was a version of the P38 manufactured by FN. No completed guns are known but the allied forces captured a large number of receivers and slides when they moved into Belgium. One important warning, apart from the usual remarks regarding wartime production, is that the P38 can be assembled and fired without the locking block. This means that the weapon functions as a blowback one and consequently serious damage will occur as well as the obvious danger.

Production of the P38 stopped in 1945 and was resumed in 1957 for the Bundeswehr. A parallel prewar development was a hammerless version which was called the Armeepistole. This weapon was not produced in quantity as the German Command chose the P38 ; Walther stopped development and production of the Armeepistole to concentrate on the P38. The Armeepistole was made with light alloy components, long barrels and even shoulder stocks during its development. When the post-war production of the P38 was resumed the weapon was made with very few modifications, although it must be noted that many post-war parts cannot be interchanged with those of the wartime production because of slight dimensional changes.

Hi-Power

A final wartime pistol that was designed but never produced was the so-called Walther Hi-Power. This was an attempt to produce a weapon not requiring the complicated forging needed in the slide and receiver of the normal automatic pistol by replacing them with simple steel stampings. The weapon has a rotating barrel similar to the Steyr

The first Mauser-produced P38 byf 42 code (*Warren H. Buxton*)

A Walther P38 produced in 1945 with the code svw 45. Notice the French proof mark (*Warren H. Buxton*)

An ac45 coded P38 reworked by the East Germans post-war. Notice the East German daisy stamp (*Warren H. Buxton*)

Standard Ulm produced commercial P38 (*Bowman*)

and a simple receiver forging with the steel stampings attached. This weapon was designed too late in the war to be produced, but emphasised the basic need, in a combat weapon, for ease of production from both cost and use of machine tools.

Flare Pistols

A further weapon produced by Walther, which must come within the scope of any history of their hand guns, is the flare pistol. The Walther flare pistol fulfils more than the name indicates as it was used to fire high explosive grenades. The pistol was designed in 1926 and adopted by the German Army in 1928, and was progressively modified as the war changed the requirements.

The basic models shows the careful design and construction expected from Walther, having such features as a rebound hammer (this prevents a blow on the hammer firing the gun or it firing when the action is being closed) ; an ejector for the spent cases, and construction which does not rely on screws to hold it together. The two grenades, which could be launched from the pistol, were a small high explosive mortar type bomb and a standard egg grenade.

As, in any military situation, there was a shortage of materials, so Walther were requested to replace steel with aluminium. To judge from the number still in existence this aluminium model would seem to have been produced in very large quantities. It can

A current production model
P38/2. This weapon has minor
changes from the standard P38
(*Warren H. Buxton*)

Right side of Ulm produced P38
showing date stamp and the
'Made in West Germany' legend
(*Bowman*)

One of the ultra-rare ac44 coded P38's
with the slide manufactured by Fabrique
Nationale. This pistol had the code
stamped by FN but was assembled by
Mauser (*Warren H. Buxton*)

A limited production post-
war.Ulm produced P38 with
a single line slide legend
(*Warren H. Buxton*)

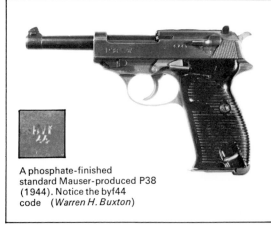

A phosphate-finished
standard Mauser-produced P38
(1944). Notice the byf44
code (*Warren H. Buxton*)

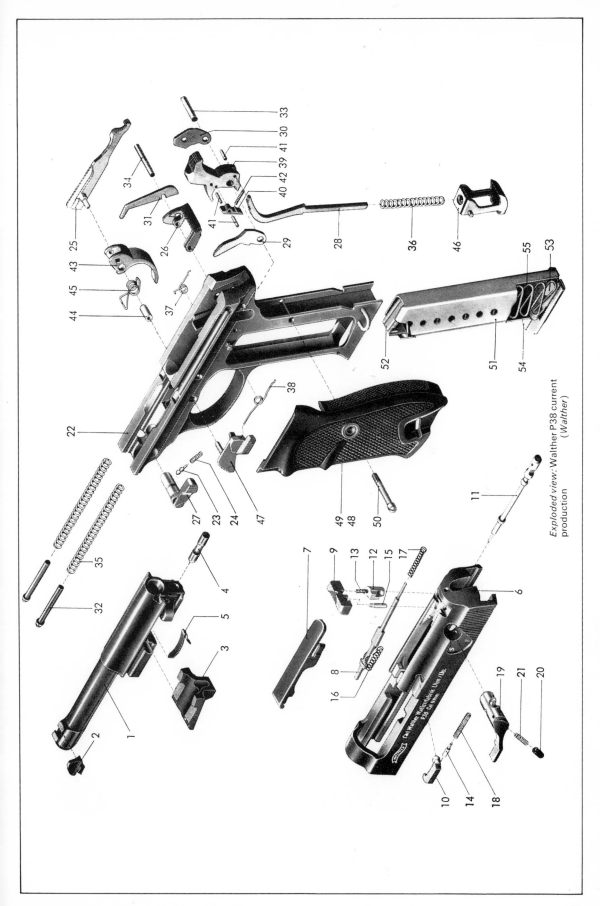

Exploded view: Walther P38 current production (*Walther*)

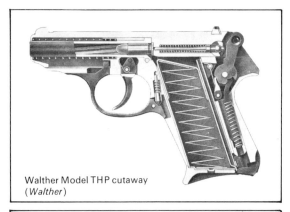

Walther Model THP cutaway
(*Walther*)

Walther Model TP. Notice the very small
size compared with the hand   (*Walther*)

Walther single barrel flare pistol with the
breech open   (*Pattern Room Enfield*)

be found with the code 237, indicating that it was
also produced by Mauser. There were a number of
alterations made to this design and it was also
produced in these modified forms by Erma (code afy)
and Berliner-Lubecker (code duv).

Towards the end of the war there were two further
modifications. The first was a change to zinc
instead of aluminium, and the second was to
improve the weapon's grenade-launching
capabilities by giving it a rifled barrel and a sighting
device on the side of the receiver. A number of high
explosive grenades and smoke bombs were issued
for use with this weapon ; it was named the
Kampfpistole. A derivation of this weapon,
specially as a portable grenade-launcher, was made
called the Sturmpistole. Also produced was a
double-barrelled flare pistol which started
production in the '30s and was adopted by the
German Navy during the war. The post-war production of the rebuilt Erma firm is an almost identical
weapon to the original. This weapon is now the
standard flare pistol of the East German Army—a
plagiarism that can only be a tribute to the original
design.

After World War II when the Walther factory was
razed to the ground, the designing and building of
calculators was resumed in the village of Wurtenberg.
This resulted in the building of a new factory at
Niederstatzingen with the most up-to-date plant

and equipment. It is here that the design of the
Walther adding machine by Georg Walther became,
along with the licence built Manhurin Pistols, a
major part in the rebuilding of the Walther factory,
post-war, culminating in the building of a further
factory at Gerstetten.

TP and TPH

Two post-war pistols which are within the scope of
this Profile (i.e. not pistols specifically for target
shooting) are the TP and the TPH. The Walther
company had had much demand for a small defence
pistol, similar to their Models 8 and 9, and so they
modified two existing designs. The TP is an updated
version of the Model 9, having the same exposed
barrel, recoil spring and method of dismantling.
The TPH is a combination of the best features of the
PP and PPK in a small pocket pistol. It has the
double action trigger of its larger brothers and it is,
like the TP, available in both ·22LF and ·25ACP.
The Walther Company still manufactures target
arms both pistols and also, like the founder
Carl Walther, top line target rifles.
It will be seen that four of the wartime production
weapons are once again in production by Walther or
other companies. These facts alone indicate that the
original creed of good design and excellent
workmanship have been fully carried out.

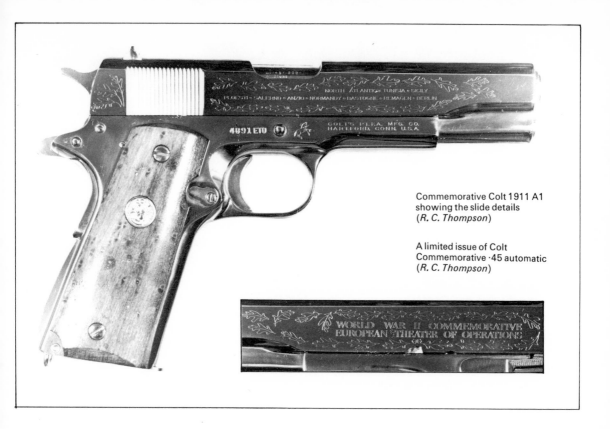

Commemorative Colt 1911 A1
showing the slide details
(*R. C. Thompson*)

A limited issue of Colt
Commemorative ·45 automatic
(*R. C. Thompson*)

The Colt ·45 Automatic and its Development

by A. J. R. Cormack

The Colt ·45 has had a love-hate relationship with its users since its arrival was announced in 1905. Love, because it will fire continuously in the worst combat conditions and give 100% stopping power; hate because of the heavy twisting recoil that makes the rookie gun-shy if not carefully trained. Its accuracy when 'tuned' by an expert is improbably good for a service side-arm. The Colt ·45 has been in service with US Forces in two World Wars, through the Korean crisis, and is in use in Vietnam as the firm favourite of the GI. It has been copied by many arms manufacturers all over the world and is used in combat by many nations today.
Any history of the Colt must start with the story of John Moses Browning. Browning was born in Utah, USA in 1855 and after working with Winchester, where he designed a number of guns, he left them following a disagreement. The history of Browning followed that of George Luger, in that Browning had to leave the USA before he received the commercial success that was his due, although, unlike Luger, Browning did return before World War I to help with weapon design. Browning joined Fabrique Nationale d'Armes de Guerre, (FN), in Belgium, where he designed the first of his long line of auto-pistols. (For details of Browning's FN designs see Profile No. 2.)
John Browning, who died in 1926, must go down in history as the most successful designer of small-arms, as his designs or their derivatives are still in front line service in most parts of the world.

Model of 1900
In 1896 Colt purchased four designs from Browning, which were to be the start of a long line of successful auto-pistols. As Colt were already the supplier of the ·38 service revolver, they were in no hurry to bring out a design which being new and untried could be branded as unreliable.
This resulted in a delay until 1900 when Colt brought out the Colt Model 1900 with a new cartridge, the ·38 Colt Automatic Cartridge or ·38 ACP. Colt named the weapon the 1900 Sporting Model.
The cartridge itself was noteworthy, in that it was the first high velocity small calibre issued to the American Army. The ·38 revolver bullet which had been used only produced a velocity of 750fps, whereas the Colt produced a hitherto unheard of 1260fps.

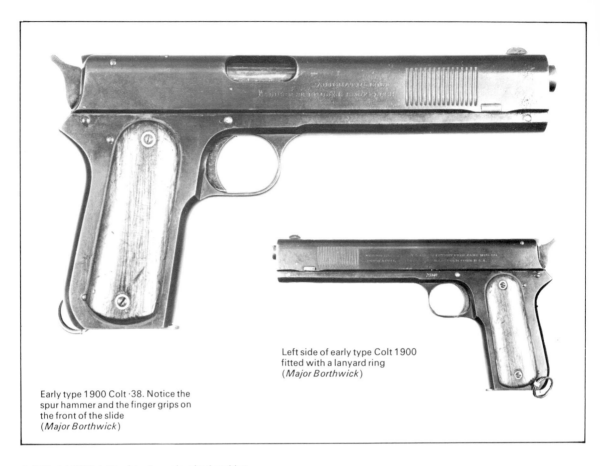

Early type 1900 Colt ·38. Notice the
spur hammer and the finger grips on
the front of the slide
(*Major Borthwick*)

Left side of early type Colt 1900
fitted with a lanyard ring
(*Major Borthwick*)

Colt Model 1900 sight safety shown in raised position
(*Major Borthwick*)

Colt Model 1900 sight safety in safe position
(*Major Borthwick*)

Colt Model 1900 fitted with a later type 1902 rounded hammer
and moulded grips   (*Pattern Room Enfield*)

The 1900 model was a seven-shot, recoil operated, locked breech weapon of excellent design and finish. The weapon had a 6in. barrel and weighed 35oz. It was the first successful use of the system using locking ribs on the barrel, which fit into corresponding ones on the slide and are pulled out of engagement on recoil by links. The difference between the link system of the Colt weapons up till the 1911 model is that a link is used at either end of the barrel as opposed to a single link after 1911. The only weakness in this and all subsequent models designed until the 1911 was that the slide is removed backwards and only held during operation by a small metal slide stop. Although there is no reason to suspect the reliability of this part, the guns should under no circumstances be fired with ·38 Super ammunition or before the slide stop has been inspected, because, if the stop fails, the slide will come rearward off the receiver into the firer's face.

An interesting safety device was employed in that the rear sight folded down and blocked the hammer from the firing pin. The finger grooves on the slide are at the rear and the grips are of plain walnut. The US Army purchased 200 in 1900 ; the pistols all bear the mark US on the left trigger guard. A very few pistols were purchased by the US Navy and were stamped 'USN' on the left frame, and the Neptune trident on the right frame.

The standard markings show the patent date—'BROWNING'S PATENT' PAT'D APRIL 20, 1897 and the calibre—'AUTOMATIC COLT CALIBRE 38 RIMLESS SMOKELESS'. As less than 3000 of these weapons were manufactured they are collector's pieces.

At the end of the 1900 production a number of features which were to appear on the 1902 model

were tried out. The illustration shows a weapon with the serrations on the slide on the front, a rounded hammer, and 1902 grips.

Sporting Model of 1902

This weapon was a modified version of the 1900 featuring the removal of the sight safety device and the use of a shorter floating firing-pin which had to be struck a full blow by the hammer to fire the cartridge. A rounded hammer, as opposed to the spur type on the Model 1900 (although on at least one or two the spur hammer was retained) was fitted and on the

Colt Military Model 1902 early version with the rounded hammer and checkered slide grip (*Pattern Room Enfield*)

An early type Military Model 1902 showing the lanyard ring and the slide hold-open device (*Pattern Room Enfield*)

early production the finger grooves were moved to the front of the slide. On the later production the patent date was changed to—'PATENTED APR. 20, 1897 SEPT 9, 1902'.

1902 Military Model

Colt, obviously with a potential military market in mind, announced the ·38 ACP Military Model (the military were at last thinking about automatic pistols) which had the following improvements or changes—one round more in the magazine, a lanyard ring, a longer squared grip and, more important, a hold open on the slide when the gun was empty. The weight was now 37oz and the weapon production continued until 1928 with more than 18,000 produced. On early weapons the slide was grooved at the front and a rounded hammer used. In 1908 modifications were introduced moving the slide grooves to the rear and a spur hammer substituted.

Colt 1902 showing the barrel locking lugs, the ejector, and an interesting 'not English made' stamp   (*Grieve*)

The corresponding cut-outs in the slide   (*Grieve*)

Right side of Colt Military Model 1902 with the 1908 modifications (*Pattern Room Enfield*)

The slide lock in its lock position with the slide rearwards (*Grieve*)

Military Model 1902 showing the spur hammer and the finger grips at the rear of the slide

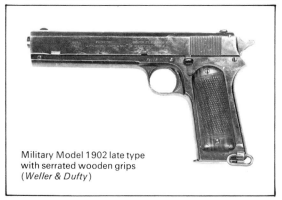

Military Model 1902 late type with serrated wooden grips (*Weller & Dufty*)

Colt Model 1902 field stripped. Notice the locking pin which is the only method of retaining the slide (*Grieve*)

Pocket Model of 1903

A pocket model with a more practical barrel length was announced in 1903. It had a 4½in barrel against a 6in one allowing the gun to be shortened from 9in to 7½in and the weight reduced to 31oz. The early production weapons had a rounded hammer with a spur used on latter ones.

During the Spanish-American War there were complaints that the ·38 revolver bullet was ineffective, leading the US Government to the conclusion that more stopping power was needed. The two calibres considered were ·41 and ·45 of which the latter was chosen. Before the 1906 Government Pistol Test the choice of a ·45 revolver round or a ·45 automatic round, both of which had been designed by the Government Ordnance Department at Frankfurt Arsenal, was given. The round chosen by Colt was the ·45 automatic round which was similar to, but longer than, the round already developed for the commercial sale of the Model 1905. The difference in length between the cases makes the rounds non-interchangeable.

It is an odd quirk of fate that the round finally adopted after various experiments was a derivation of the Colt commercial round and not the Government designed one.

Left side of the Pocket Model 1903. This is an early production weapon with a rounded hammer (*Pattern Room Enfield*)

Left side of a Pocket Model 1903 early type (*Pattern Room Enfield*)

John Browning was, by this time, back with his old company, Winchester, where in collaboration with them and the Army, he finalised the design of the 1911 ·45 automatic cartridge.

Military Model of 1905

The gun to fire the new commercial ·45 round was an enlarged ·38 Military model of 1902 and has the same slide lock. Although there were only 6000 or so of the 1905 Colts sold, these included 400 to the Army in 1907. The weapons for the 1906 tests were rechambered for the Government ·45 round. The 1905 once again had the slide stop as the only method of retaining the slide during recoil.

The barrel was 5in long and as with the Sporting Model of 1903 the balance of the weapon was improved. The author has found the 1902 model with the 6in barrel very muzzle heavy and thus tending to point low when fired in a hurry.

As the patent for this weapon was not granted before December 1905 the patent dates on the slide are as on the 1902 models but after December they were—'PATENTED APR. 20, 1897, SEPT. 9, 1902, DEC. 19, 1905'. The right hand side of the slide is marked—'AUTOMATIC COLT CALIBRE ·45 RIMLESS SMOKELESS'.

Military Model of 1911

This was to be the turning point for the auto-pistol and for Browning. The Army were so impressed

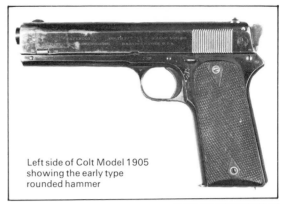

Left side of Colt Model 1905 showing the early type rounded hammer

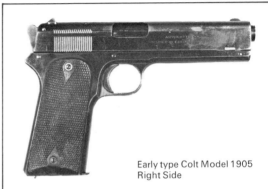

Early type Colt Model 1905 Right Side

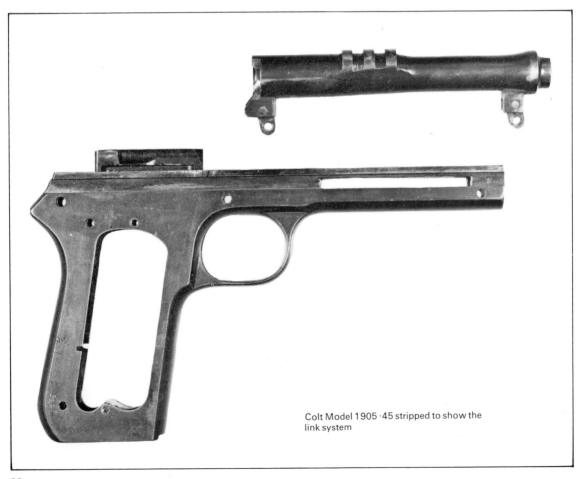

Colt Model 1905 ·45 stripped to show the link system

A cased .45 Colt World War II Commemorative Thompson.

Left side of late type Colt 1905
showing lanyard ring and late type
spur hammer
(*Pattern Room Enfield*)

Right side of late type Colt 1905
showing clearly the slide markings
(*Pattern Room Enfield*)

that they encouraged Colt and Browning to develop
the ·45 automatic into a combat weapon.
The modifications which were carried out by
Browning were the strengthening of the magazine,
a grip and subsequently a manual safety (as a grip
safety was not used by Browning on all of his
designs it may have been at the insistence of the
Army), a spur hammer, and the uprating of the 1905
commercial cartridge by increasing the bullet weight
from 200 to 230 grains. With the uprating of the
cartridge and a need to strengthen the gun,
Browning took the opportunity to change the slide
stop which was the main weakness and redesign
the twin barrel links to the single one of the Model
1911. These modifications appeared in a number of
experimental pistols, each of which tried out and
often rejected new features. The Model 1911 was,
therefore, a completely redesigned pistol although a
logical development.
These changes led to the successful adoption of the
Colt 1911 by the American Army. The trials included
the Savage and the Luger amongst others, so it was
not without strong opposition that the Colt finally
won through.
During World War I the British were forced to buy
supplementary arms from the United States and as
one of the cartridges employed by the British was
the ·455 Auto (used in the Webley Auto-Pistol) the
Colt 1911 was chambered for this cartridge. Owing
to differences in cartridge dimension the ·455 Auto
will not chamber in the ·45 ACP, and although
possible to fire the ·45 ACP in the ·455 Auto this is
not recommended because of the excessive head
space. The bore dimensions are very similar.

Left side of the Author's
Model 1911 showing clearly
the patent dates and the
interesting British and
G2 markings

The Author's own Model 1911
which was produced by Colt in
1914

Model 1911 A1

The next and final modifications were to bring the
gun up to the Model 1911 A1 ; these were done in
1921. The modifications were, in fact, interchangeable with the earlier model. The rear of the
grip was arched and checkered, the trigger and
trigger guard altered, an easier to use safety device

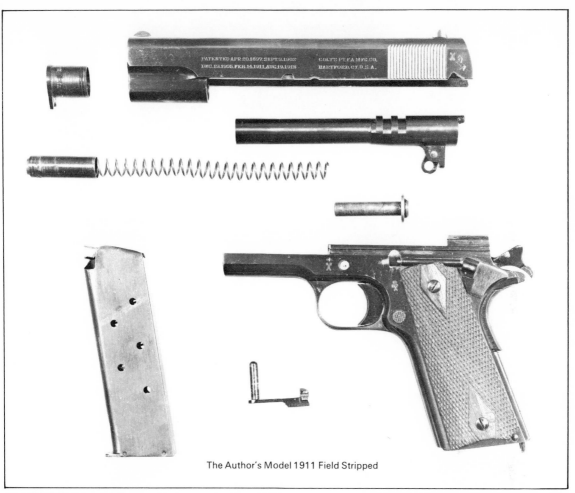

The Author's Model 1911 Field Stripped

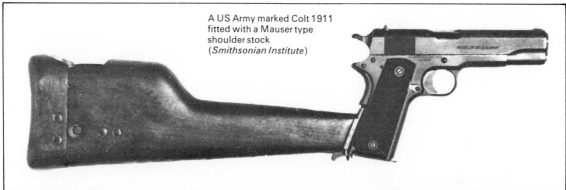

A US Army marked Colt 1911 fitted with a Mauser type shoulder stock (*Smithsonian Institute*)

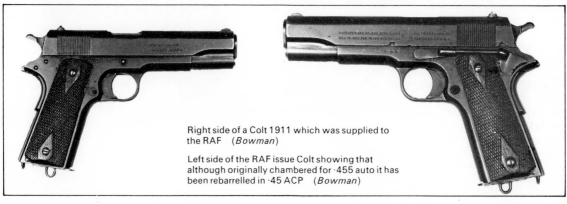

Right side of a Colt 1911 which was supplied to the RAF   (*Bowman*)

Left side of the RAF issue Colt showing that although originally chambered for ·455 auto it has been rebarrelled in ·45 ACP   (*Bowman*)

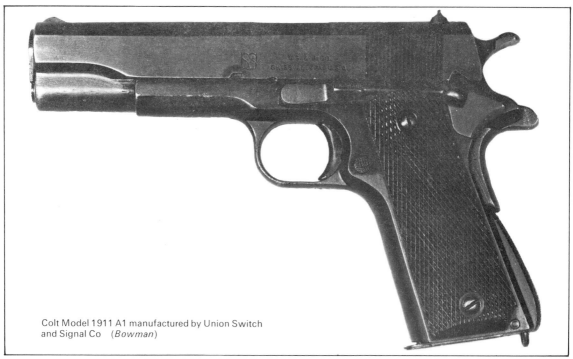

Colt Model 1911 A1 manufactured by Union Switch
and Signal Co   (*Bowman*)

Slide markings from 1911 A1   (*Pattern Room Enfield*)

and finally a change in the shape of the hammer. The
original 1911 continued until 1913 when the new
Patent by Browning simplified the design by
reducing the total number of parts used. This is of
great importance when the following is considered.
A standard 1911 of the latter type has 728 machining
operations with 187 checks and inspections !
The Patent Markings are as follows—'PATENTED
APR. 20, 1897, SEPT. 9, 1902, DEC. 19, 1905,
FEB. 14, 1911' and after changes in 1913
'AUG. 19, 1913' was added.
During the life of the Colt, and particularly during
World Wars I and II it has been manufactured by
Remington Rand Co, Union Switch and Signal Co,
Remington Arms Co, Ithica Gun Co, North American
Arms Co Ltd, and Singer Sewing Machine Co.
There were more than 2,500,000 units
manufactured before the end of World War II.

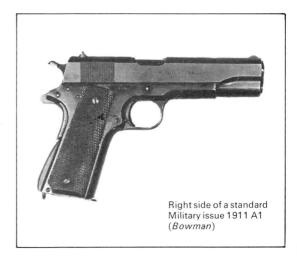

Right side of a standard
Military issue 1911 A1
(*Bowman*)

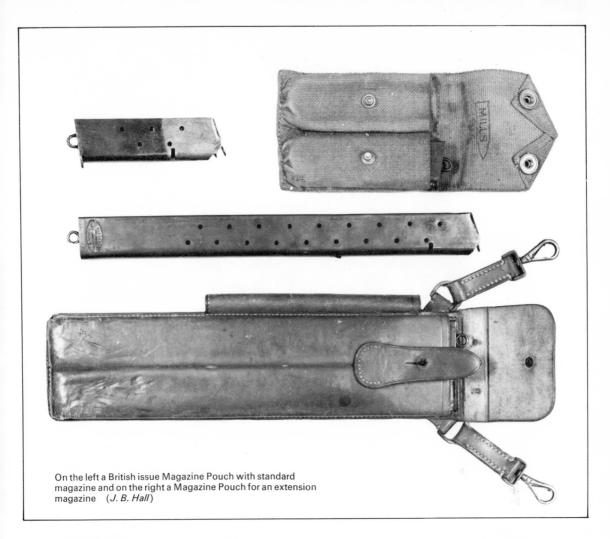

On the left a British issue Magazine Pouch with standard magazine and on the right a Magazine Pouch for an extension magazine (*J. B. Hall*)

Mk. IV Series 70 Government Model

The one disadvantage with the locking system encountered in the standard weapons of this type, is the method of lining up the barrel at the muzzle end. There has to be a certain amount of free play as the barrel has to drop to unlock. This free play as the author has experienced, ranges from a good fit (just enough to allow the gun to function) to the barrel floating about $\frac{1}{16}$in. Many gunsmiths have used their own special bushes to replace the factory one, but most have had trouble with unreliable functioning. The Colt factory have solved the problem by using a four fingered bush bearing on a swelling on the barrel end. This method will become standard eventually on all production Colt ·45 Autos as it has on the Mk IV Series '70 and the Gold Cup. As yet the parts are not available to convert the older weapons, but this can only be a matter of time. A large number of variations and derivatives of the 1911 A1 have been made with the intention of improving the basic gun for specific applications. They are as follows:

Colt National Match
and Gold Cup National Match

Target shooters demanded a more accurate version of the standard weapon and this weapon was provided by a number of specialist gunsmiths.

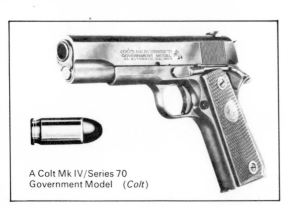

A Colt Mk IV/Series 70 Government Model (*Colt*)

Diagram of the Series 70 Barrel Bushing (*Colt*)

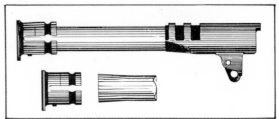

The right side of the European Commemmorative
with the Colt Medallion inset into the grip *Thompson*

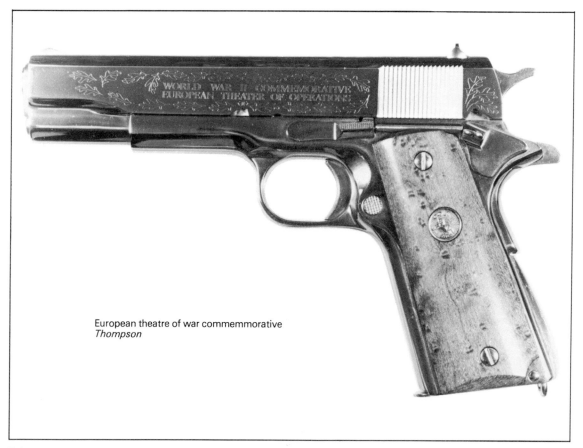

European theatre of war commemmorative
Thompson

The Colt Series 70 Gold Cup National Match   (*Colt*)

full load ammunition as there is a considerable increase in the recoil. Many authorities consider it good advice to fire light loads for practice and only the full loads for combat use. This will also save the alloy receiver from undue wear (this does not indicate any lack of strength, but alloy receivers do wear out more quickly than their steel counterparts). Production started in 1959 and it is a current production line, being offered additionally in 9mm parabellum and ·38 Super. The Commander is 8in long and has a barrel length of $4\frac{1}{4}$in.

The latest All Steel Colt Combat Commander   (*Colt*)

Colt, realising that this could be a lucrative market, decided to produce a weapon to fill the gap. The result was the Gold Cup, which was announced in 1933, and was a meticulously assembled 1911 A1, with target sights, on the later production. Manufacture was terminated during World War II and when it was resumed in 1957 the weapon was renamed the Gold Cup National Match. The only major modification was the addition of a wider grooved trigger with a trigger stop.

With the introduction of the Mk IV Series '70 barrel bushing, the Gold Cup National Match was updated to include the bush. The dimensions of the model 0-5 are length $8\frac{1}{2}$in with a barrel of 5in and a weight of 37oz.

Colt Commander

This weapon is the result of a request for a lighter weapon to fire the ·45 ACP cartridge. The receiver and main spring housing are machined from a Coltalloy forging. This is a high tensile light alloy which, combined with a $\frac{3}{4}$in shorter barrel, gives a weight reduction from 39oz to $26\frac{1}{2}$oz. This reduction in weight makes the weapon difficult to fire with

Combat Commander

In 1971 the Colt Company after many requests decided to market an all steel version of the Commander. This weapon they named the Combat Commander. It features the same dimensions as the Commander but being all steel now weighs 33oz. This addition means that the weapon will not suffer the same wear as would the present when heavy loads are fired from the alloy version.

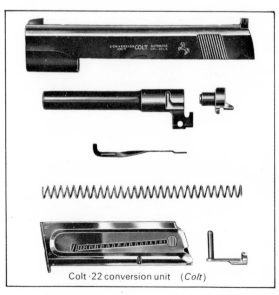

A Colt Commander chambered for the 9mm Luger cartridge. This is also available in ·45 (*Colt*)

Colt ·22 conversion unit   (*Colt*)

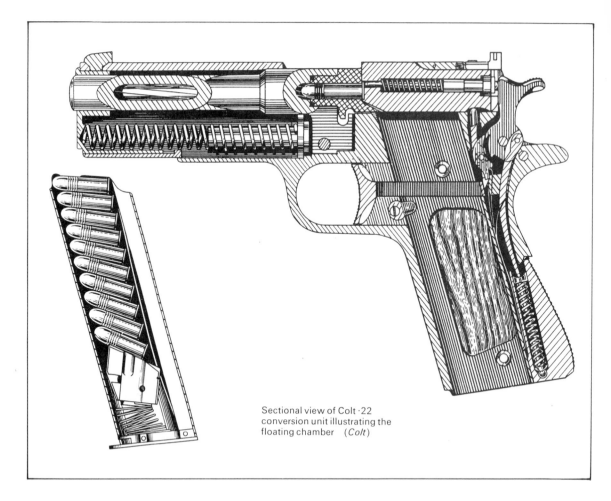

Sectional view of Colt ·22 conversion unit illustrating the floating chamber   (*Colt*)

As would be expected a number of small bore ·22 Long Rifle conversions were made for the Colt ·45. Only the official Colt conversions are enumerated here :

ACE ·22 (O-22)
In 1931 Colt, after a number of unsuccessful attempts, announced a cheap to fire practice conversion chambered for the ·22 long rifle cartridge. This weapon was not issued as a kit, but as a complete weapon. It operated on the blowback system on a standard receiver.

ACE SERVICE ·22 (O-SM)
One disadvantage with a simple ·22 LR conversion in training is the lack of recoil and thus D. M. Williams devised a boosted blowback. The booster is a floating chamber which is recessed into the rear of the barrel and has the chamber in it. When the gun is fired the chamber moves backwards—allowing the gases to exert pressure against the front face of the chamber which, because of its greater area than the cartridge, increases the recoil four times. Once again this was not issued as a conversion but as a complete weapon, thus giving a need for the rarest conversion of them all, the ·45 ACP conversion for the ·22LR. The Ace ·22LR was brought out in 1937 and continued in production until 1941 although some were assembled as late as 1947. The current conversion is issued as a complete slide,

having Colt's Accro target sights. A special magazine is issued and the parts are directly replaceable on the standard receiver. Once again the boosted blowback is used giving a four times greater recoil than with standard ·22 long rifle ammunition.

Argentinian Colts
Although a great number of copies of the Colt have been manufactured, the Argentinian produced weapons are unusual, in that they were built under licence. The Argentinian Government decided on the Colt ·45 as standard issue and purchased large numbers from the States.

Colt Model 1916
This weapon is a standard, commercially numbered 1911 Colt. The standard Colt numbers and markings are supplemented by Seal of Argentine on the top of the slide and an extra serial number.

Colt Model 1927
When the 1911 A1 became a standard production the Argentinian Government ordered more weapons from Colt's commercial production. The markings are similar to those of the Model 1916 but the slide markings are duplicated in Spanish.

Systems Colt
This weapon is identical and fully interchangeable with the standard 1911 A1. The Argentinian

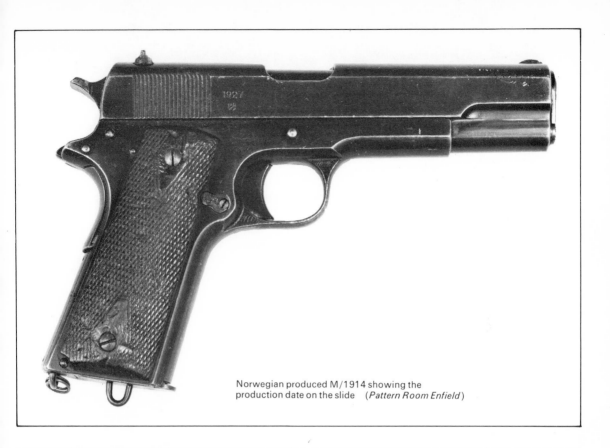

Norwegian produced M/1914 showing the
production date on the slide   (*Pattern Room Enfield*)

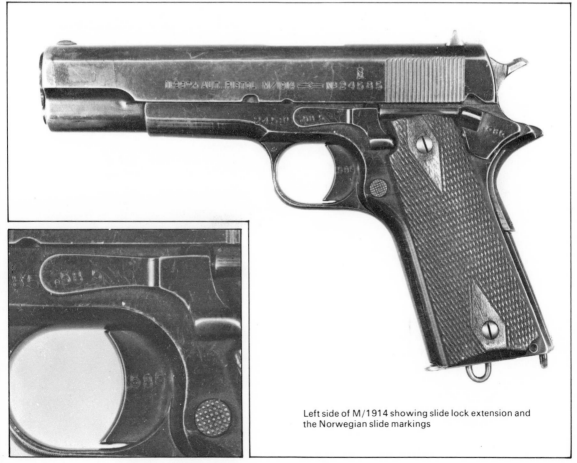

Left side of M/1914 showing slide lock extension and
the Norwegian slide markings

Ballester-Molina. This is a Colt copy. Notice the
deletion of the magazine safety
(*Pattern Room Enfield*)

Government installed machinery licenced from
Colt at the Government Controlled Arsenal of
Fabrica Militar d'Armes Pontatiles and manufactured the 1911 A1 under direct licences from Colt.
The final weapon manufactured in the Argentine
was not a Colt but one of many derivations which
have been produced throughout the world. This is
detailed under Colt copies.

Norwegian M/1912 and M/1914

The only other real Colts produced outside the
United States other than the various copies, were
the result of the Norwegian Government testing a
number of pistols in 1909-1912. Colt delivered
300 standard 1911 pistols before the outbreak of
the First World War stopped delivery. The
Norwegians decided to manufacture the weapon

The Author's Star which once again is a copy of the
Colt with the grip safety deleted

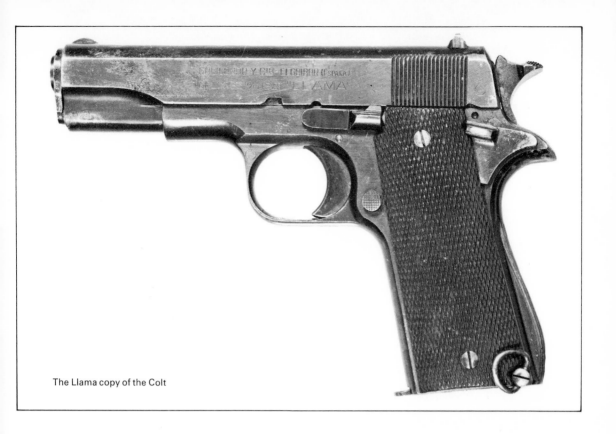

The Llama copy of the Colt

themselves and an initial batch was produced at the Government-owned Kongsberg Weapons Factory. There were 500 produced between 1917 and 1919, serial numbered 1 onwards. In 1914 the slide stop had the finger piece lengthened. The production is presumed to have stopped during the Second World War, as after the War the Norwegians purchased the standard Model from the USA. These weapons were all chambered for the 11·25mm cartridge which is identical to the ·45 ACP.

Colt Copies

As there have been a large number of Colt copies only three representative weapons will be covered.
'Hafdasa' Ballester-Molina—This weapon is a simplified 1911 A1 without the grip safety. It was manufactured for Hafdasa in Buenos Aires, by Ballester-Molina who are no longer in business.
Star Model B—On this Spanish-made weapon the action and outside appearance are identical to the Colt, only lacking the grip safety. The stripping of the weapon is carried out in an identical manner to the 1911 A1. The finish is not up to the high standard of the Colt.
Llama—Another Spanish weapon with, unlike the above, a grip safety but otherwise identical with the Star. Again the fine finish is lacking.

It now looks as if this old war horse will never die as no successor has been adopted. The continuous use as the standard American side arm for 60 years is the only tribute necessary to the genius of J. M. Browning.

A late production Sporting Model 1902 with spur hammer and checkered wood grips
(*Pattern Room Enfield*)

UNITED STATES MILITARY SERIAL NUMBERS FOR 1911, 1911A1 ·45 AUTOMATICS

Year	Serial Numbers	Manufacturer
1912	1-500	Colt
	501-1000	Colt USN
	1001-1500	Colt
	1501-2000	Colt USN
	2001-2500	Colt
	2501-3500	Colt USN
	3501-3800	Colt USMC
	3801-4500	Colt
	4501-5500	Colt USN
	5501-6500	Colt
	6501-7500	Colt USN
	7501-8500	Colt
	8501-9500	Colt USN
	9501-10500	Colt
	10501-11500	Colt USN
	11501-12500	Colt
	12501-13500	Colt USN
	13501-17250	Colt
1913	17251-36400	Colt
	36401-37650	Colt USMC
	37651-38000	Colt
	38001-44000	Colt USN
	44001-60400	Colt

Year	Serial Numbers	Manufacturer	Year	Serial Numbers	Manufacturer
1914	60401-72570	Colt	1918	232001-233600	Colt USN
	72571-83855	Springfield—(These numbers reserved for Springfield product)		233601-594000	Colt
				1-13152	Rem. UMC
	83856-83900	Colt	1919	13153-21676	Rem. UMC
	83901-84400	Colt USMC		594001-629500	Colt
	84401-96000	Colt		629501-700000	Unknown
	96001-97537	Colt	1924	700001-710000	Colt
	97538-102596	Colt	1937	710001-712349	Colt
	102597-107596	Springfield—(Reserved for Springfield product)	1938	712350-713645	Colt
			1939	713646-717281	Colt USN
1915	107597-109500	Colt	1940	717282-721977	Colt
	109501-110000	Colt USN	1941	721978-756733	Colt
	110001-113496	Colt	1942	756734-800000	Colt
	113497-120566	Springfield—(Reserved for Springfield product)		S800001-S800600	Singer
	120567-125566	Colt		800501-801000	These numbers assigned to H & R
	125567-133186	Springfield—(Reserved for Springfield product)	1943	801001-958100	Colt
				958101-1088725	US & S
1916	133187-137400	Colt		1088726-1208673	Colt
1917	137401-151186	Colt		1208674-1279673	Ithaca
	151187-151986	Colt USMC		1279674-1279698	re no AA
	151987-185800	Colt		1279699-1441430	Remington-Rand
	185801-186200	Colt USMC		1441431-1471430	Ithaca
	186201-209586	Colt		1471431-1609528	Remington-Rand
	209587-210386	Colt USMC	1944	1609529-1743846	Colt
	210387-215386	Colt frames (Reserved for receivers and service)		1743847-1890503	Ithaca
				1890504-2075103	Remington-Rand
	215387-216186	Colt USMC	1945	2075104-2134403	Ithaca
	216187-216586	Colt		2134404-2244803	Remington-Rand
	216587-216986	Colt USMC		2244804-2380013	Colt
1918	216987-217386	Colt USMC		2380014-2619013	Remington-Rand
	217387-232000	Colt		2619014-2693613	Ithaca
				to 1957 numbers remarked to X2695212	

SPECIFICATION

MODEL	LENGTH	BARREL LENGTH	CALIBRE	MAGAZINE CAPACITY	WEIGHT
Model 1900	9·00″	6·00″	·38	7	35oz
Sporting Model 1902	9·00″	6·00″	·38	7	35oz
1902 Military Model	9·00″	6·00″	·38	8	37oz
Pocket Model of 1903	7·5″	4·5″	·38	7	31oz
Military Model of 1905	8·00″	5·00″	·45	7	Early Model 32½oz Late Model 34oz
Military Model of 1911	8·5″	5·00″	·45 ACP	7	39oz
Colt Commander	8·00″	4·25″	·45 ACP ·38 ACP 9mm	7—·45 ACP 9—·38 SUPER 9—9mm PARA	26½oz
Combat Commander	8·00″	4·25″	·45 ACP ·38 ACP 9mm	7—·45 ACP 9—·38 SUPER 9—9mm PARA	33oz

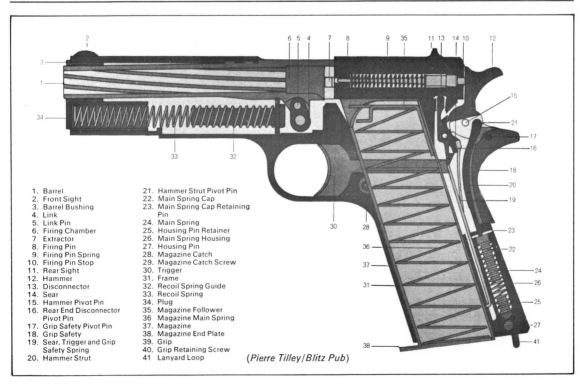

1. Barrel
2. Front Sight
3. Barrel Bushing
4. Link
5. Link Pin
6. Firing Chamber
7. Extractor
8. Firing Pin
9. Firing Pin Spring
10. Firing Pin Stop
11. Rear Sight
12. Hammer
13. Disconnector
14. Sear
15. Hammer Pivot Pin
16. Rear End Disconnector Pivot Pin
17. Grip Safety Pivot Pin
18. Grip Safety
19. Sear, Trigger and Grip Safety Spring
20. Hammer Strut
21. Hammer Strut Pivot Pin
22. Main Spring Cap
23. Main Spring Cap Retaining Pin
24. Main Spring
25. Housing Pin Retainer
26. Main Spring Housing
27. Housing Pin
28. Magazine Catch
29. Magazine Catch Screw
30. Trigger
31. Frame
32. Recoil Spring Guide
33. Recoil Spring
34. Plug
35. Magazine Follower
36. Magazine Main Spring
37. Magazine
38. Magazine End Plate
39. Grip
40. Grip Retaining Screw
41. Lanyard Loop

(Pierre Tilley/Blitz Pub)

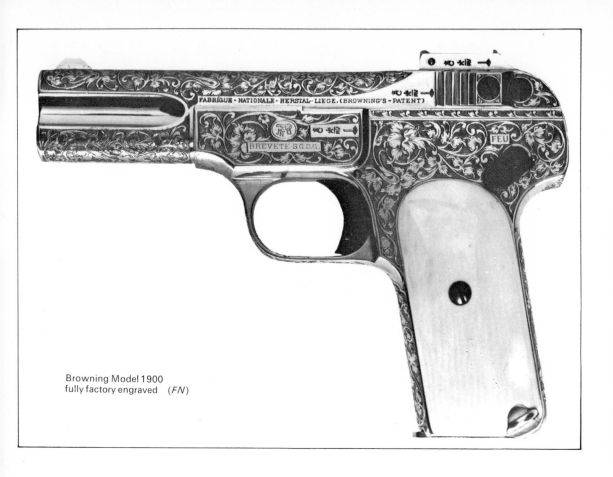

Browning Model 1900
fully factory engraved (*FN*)

Browning Automatic Pistols and the Hi-Power

by A. J. R. Cormack

The histories of J. M. Browning and Fabrique Nationale have been linked since July 1897. Their combined genius has resulted in an unrivalled range of weapons, many of which are still in production and combat use. Browning's own boast, that his weapons were not equalled in the East of the United States, does not need his qualification that they might be equalled further West. John Browning was born in Ogden, Utah, in 1855, of a Mormon father, who had at an early age served as an apprentice gunsmith and who produced guns to order. It is not surprising that one of his sons should become the world's greatest and most prolific designer of firearms. One of Browning's early designs for a rifle attracted the attention of the Winchester Arms Co. of Hartford, Connecticut. Browning & Brothers produced about 600 of these rifles, whereupon Winchester, who respected Browning's designs, realised that they might also be

serious competitors! Winchester, therefore, not only bought manufacturing rights for the rifle, but also the original 600 weapons. This weapon was marketed by Winchester as their Model 1886. It was to be followed by a number of equally famous rifles and shotguns. Unfortunately for Winchester a disagreement with Browning caused him to join F.N.

It must be said that Winchester's loss was certainly F.N.'s gain. The first contract between Browning and the F.N. was signed in July 1897; it was for a small 7·65 automatic pistol and from this point the histories of Browning and Fabrique Nationale were closely linked.

The F.N. Organisation was founded in 1889 by a group of ten citizens of Liege to manufacture 150,000 1889 Mauser rifles for the Belgian Government. Encouraged by the success of this venture, the company decided to continue with

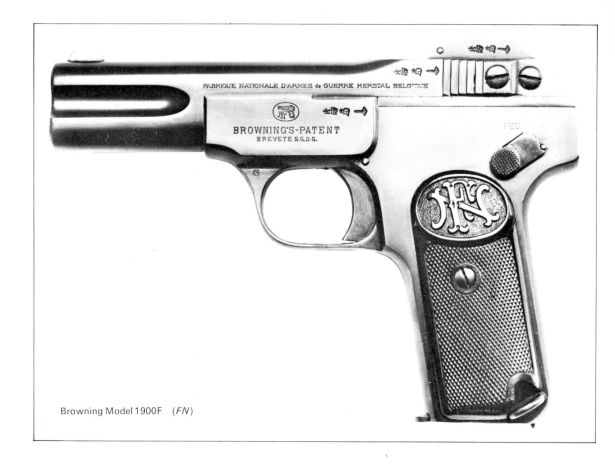

Browning Model 1900F   (*FN*)

weapon design and manufacture. The company today employs some 12,000 people in four main manufacturing divisions. Apart from the arms and cartridge factories, with which we are concerned in this Profile, there is also an engine division and a precision engineering division.

Model 1900

Browning's first design for F.N. was one of his few failures : a fully automatic pistol firing a ·38 bullet at a muzzle velocity of 1300fps. Needless to say this was uncontrollable as the successive recoils pushed the muzzle higher and higher. Although the Model 1900 was the first weapon designed by Browning to be manufactured in quantity by F.N., it was preceded by at least two weapons, one of which, patented in 1897 (No. 580924) became a basis for Colt's early production, and the other a Model 1899, which was similar to the 1900. The dimensions of the 1899 were : 7·2in. overall ; 4·8in. barrel ; weight 26·9oz. This weapon was only made in very small quantities.

The Browning Model 1900 was patented on 21 March 1899. (Patent No. 621747.) It was not surprising that, as the first successfully mass-produced pocket pistol, over 1,000,000 were sold by June 1912. As it was a straight blowback type it set the pattern which has been followed by most small automatic pistols. It also introduced the 7·65mm Browning automatic pistol cartridge (this

was a derivation of a Bergman-Simplex round which became better known as the ·32ACP). This cartridge had been introduced in the two proto-type pistols in 1898 and 1899. The one departure

Browning Model 1900
(*Bowman*)

Browning Model 1900
note the early type grip
emblem   (*FN*)

from all Browning's later designs was that the recoil spring ran parallel to and on top of the barrel. There have been a number of attempts to make copies of this weapon ranging from near exact to dangerous. If any doubt is held, the weapon's markings should be examined carefully for error.

The dimensions of the 1900 are : 6·75in. long ; 4in. barrel ; weight 22oz. The magazine capacity is 7 shots. It can be seen from the accompanying illustrations of the pistol that the exterior finish and workmanship is of an extremely high quality.

Model 1903

This pistol was used as a military weapon for some years in Belgium, Denmark and Sweden (where it is also known as the pistol Model 07) the Netherlands and Turkey. It was produced by Husqvarna for the Swedish Government and some weapons have the Husqvarna trade mark on them. It is a blowback pistol chambered for 9mm Browning long. This cartridge (also used for one of the Webley automatics) which is now obsolete, is a shortened ·38ACP but having a very much reduced load. It is

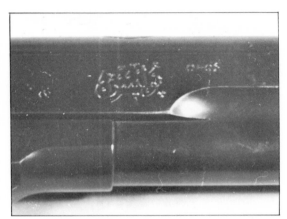

Browning Model 1903 detail—notice the Turkish markings (*Pattern Room, Enfield*)

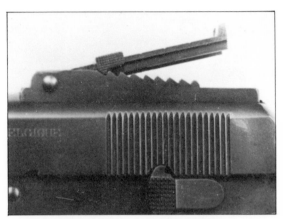

Browning Model 1903 adjustable sights   (*FN*)

Browning Model 1903 standard   (*FN*)

Browning Engraved Model 1903 notice the delicate flower pattern   (*FN*)

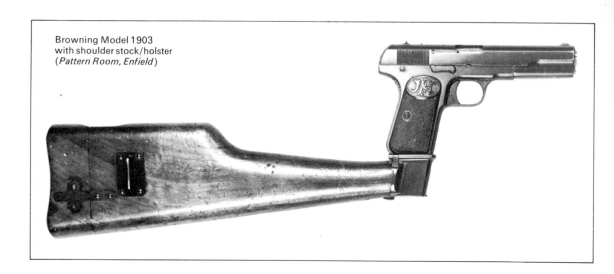

Browning Model 1903
with shoulder stock/holster
(*Pattern Room, Enfield*)

Browning Model 1903 Husqvarna trade mark

interesting to read in a review of the Model 1903 by the Belgian Army, that the subject of calibre and stopping power is given much thought. The conclusion of the report is that a calibre of at least 9mm is desirable to provide the necessary stopping power. However, the Browning 9mm long can hardly be classed as a powerful cartridge having a muzzle velocity of only 1000fps.

In many weapons of the period considerable emphasis was placed on the use of shoulder stocks. A number of illustrations show the Model 1903 with not only a shoulder stock of the Mauser type, but the gun fitted with an extension magazine. The dimensions of the 1903 are : 8in. long ; 5in. barrel ; weight 32oz. The magazine capacity is 7 shots.

Left: Browning Model 1910   (*FN*)

Right: Browning Model 1910
Fully factory engraved   (*FN*)

Model 1910

In 1910 Browning patented an improvement on the Model 1903 which did not, however, go into production until 1912. The 1910 was offered in calibres ·32ACP and ·380ACP (·390ACP is also known as 9mm Browning short or 9mm corté) and, in fact, some weapons were manufactured with matching ·380ACP and ·32ACP barrels. By 1935 F.N. had manufactured 1,000,000 pistols of this model, which is still in production today but has been renamed the Model 10. The only improvements during its long life are merely 'tidying up' of the basic design. One interesting point which was and is heavily advertised by Browning, is that the pistol has, in effect, three safeties ; the grip safety, which became a feature on a lot of Colt produced Browning designs and which prevents the pistol being fired unless a firm grip is taken of it ; an intermediate or magazine safety, which prevents the pistol being fired without the magazine in place ; and, finally, the ordinary safety which immobilises both sear and slide.

The dimensions of the 1910 ·380ACP version are : 6in. long ; 3·5in. barrel ; weight 20oz. The magazine capacity is 6 shots. ·32ACP version : weight 20·5oz. The magazine capacity is 7 shots.

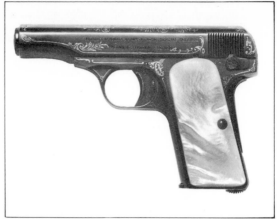

Browning Model 1910
Factory engraved with pearl handle   (*FN*)

Model 1922

In 1922 the Model 1910 was enlarged and renamed the Model 1922. Once again this was a straight blowback pistol manufactured in calibres ·32ACP

Browning Model 1922
Standard ·380 ACP   (*Henry*)

Browning Model 1922 Standard ·380 ACP   (*Henry*)

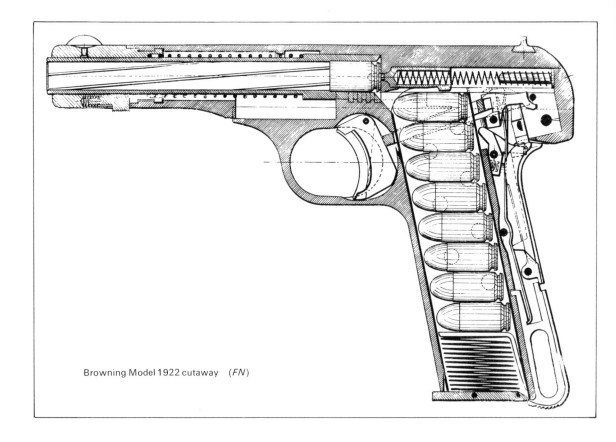

Browning Model 1922 cutaway   (*FN*)

and ·380ACP. It was designed with military use in mind as it has a greater sighting radius, a longer barrel and a larger magazine capacity. To enable the same machinery to be employed as for the 1910 an extension was fitted by means of a bayonet catch to the end of a standard 1910 slide. This weapon was adopted by the Netherlands, Yugoslavia and Belgium among others. During the occupation of Belgium by the Germans its production was continued but, as as with most weapons produced under such conditions, quality deteriorated considerably to the extent that any pistol encountered with German markings should be examined carefully before firing. The 1922 Model was dropped from F.N. production after the war but reinstated with the designation Model 10/22.

Browning Model 1922 partially stripped—notice the slide extension bayonet catch   (*Henry*)

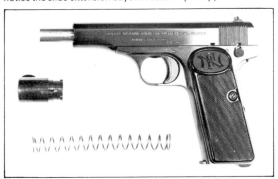

The dimensions of the 1922 ·380ACP version are : 7in. long ; 4·5in. barrel ; weight 24oz ; height 4·75in. ·32ACP version weight 24oz. The magazine capacity on the ·380ACP is 8 cartridges and on the ·32ACP 9 cartridges.

Browning Model ·25 ACP
Baby Browning   (*FN*)
Below: Baby trade mark   (*FN*)
(*Exploded illustration p. 40*)

·25ACP Browning Pistols

The first ·25ACP Browning was a miniature blowback pistol similar to the Colt Vest Pocket Model. Before production was terminated F.N. produced 4,000,000 of this model. It has be superseded by the Browning Baby. The Baby is produced in three versions. The first two are mechanically identical but the weapon retailed in Europe has the word 'Baby' moulded into the grips and the weapon marketed in the United States has merely the F.N. Monogram. The third weapon is a lightweight version of the Baby, having an alloy frame. This is only available by special order or on the United States market.

The dimensions of the first model ·25ACP are: 5in. long; 2·5in. barrel; weight 13·5oz.; with a magazine capacity of 6 cartridges. The dimensions of the Baby Browning are: 4in. long; 2·75in. high; 2·1in. barrel; weight 9·7oz. The lightweight version is identical but weighs 7·75oz. Both models have the magazine capacity of 6 cartridges. As these weapons fire ·25ACP cartridges they cannot be considered practical military weapons although men *have* been killed by this cartridge.

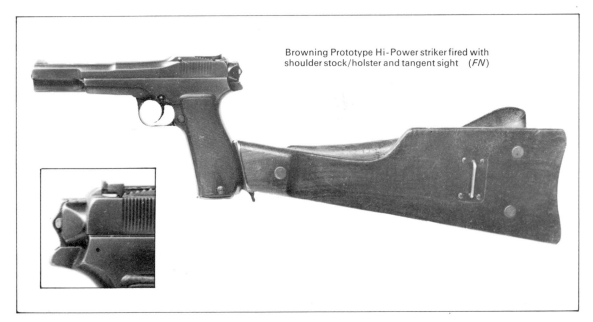

Browning Prototype Hi-Power striker fired with shoulder stock/holster and tangent sight   (*FN*)

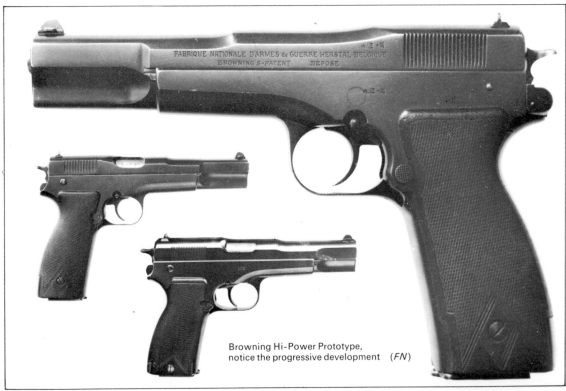

Browning Hi-Power Prototype,
notice the progressive development   (*FN*)

Model 1935 or Hi-Power

Before his death in December 1926, Browning applied for a patent for a new pistol, which was to be called the Model 1935. This patent was granted in February 1927, three months after his death.

This was to be the final simplification of the Browning designed parallel ruler locked breech. It in fact, simplified his earlier design typified by the Model 1911 Colt. With perhaps the exception of the Colt, this weapon has been the most successful of all automatic pistols, being in constant use since its formal introduction in 1935 in the British, Canadian, Danish and many other modern armies. It was extensively used during World War II by combatants on both sides.

The illustrations show that, although from prototype form to final production weapon there were a number of exterior changes, apart from the first version being a striker-fired one as opposed to the later hammer-fired weapons, there were in fact no major ones. It is once again interesting to note the use on the earlier prototypes of a shoulder stock and a tangent rear sight. This feature, in fact, was to be reintroduced at a later date. The grip safety, which had been prominent in Browning designs up to this time, was deleted and a manual safety relied upon. The Germans, after their over-running of Belgium where the weapon had been in production for some time, issued it to the S.S. and other specialist

Browning Production
Hi-Power   (*FN*)

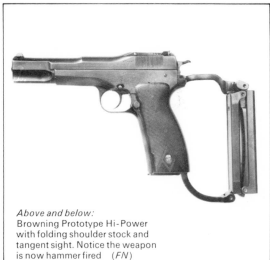

Above and below:
Browning Prototype Hi-Power with folding shoulder stock and tangent sight. Notice the weapon is now hammer fired   (*FN*)

Browning Production Hi-Power factory engraved   (*FN*)
Below: Slide release. Magazine release button. Safety catch

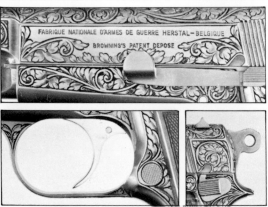

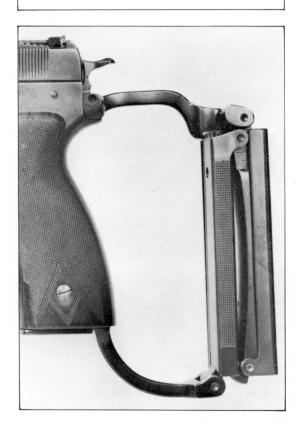

Browning Factory fully engraved Hi-Power   (*FN*)

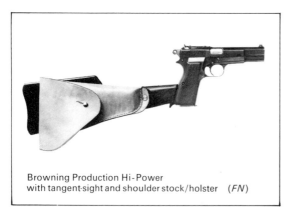

Browning Production Hi-Power
with tangent-sight and shoulder stock/holster   (*FN*)

Browning Production Hi-Power
with deluxe grips   (*FN*)

troops. This, of course, caused no logistic problems as 9mm parabellum was their standard ammunition. If a Browning is found with German proof marks it should first be checked to see that the magazine safety is fitted, as in a number of pistols manufactured under German occupation such luxuries were deleted. Earlier remarks regarding wartime produced weapons also apply. The commercial production of the Browning Hi-Power once again features some heavily engraved weapons. The Browning Hi-Power is seen on many target ranges being used for many pistol competitions. The ease with which this gun fires any of the standard service ammunitions, coupled with its reliability and ease of operation, make it an ideal pistol for any type of usage. As well as being in use by the British Army a number of police forces have adopted it for the above reasons.

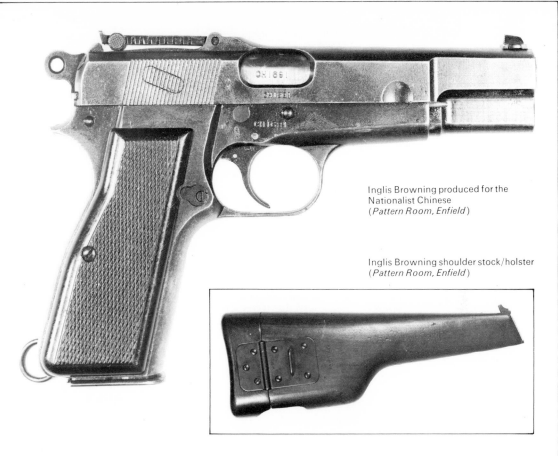

Inglis Browning produced for the
Nationalist Chinese
(*Pattern Room, Enfield*)

Inglis Browning shoulder stock/holster
(*Pattern Room, Enfield*)

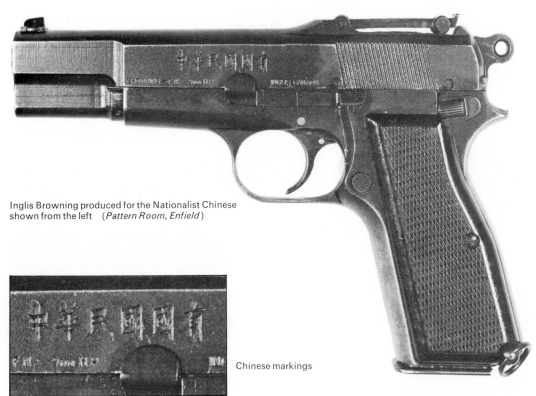

Inglis Browning produced for the Nationalist Chinese
shown from the left   (*Pattern Room, Enfield*)

Chinese markings

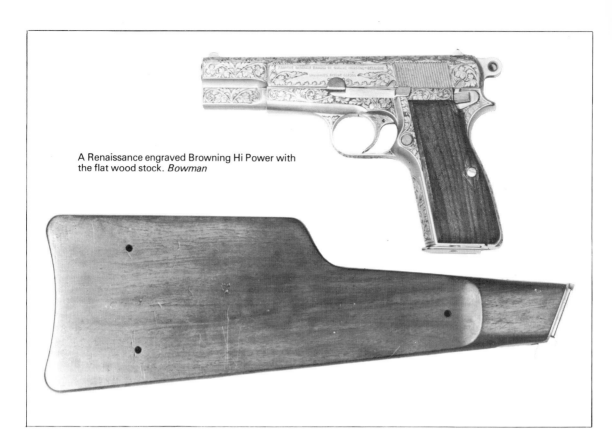

A Renaissance engraved Browning Hi Power with the flat wood stock. *Bowman*

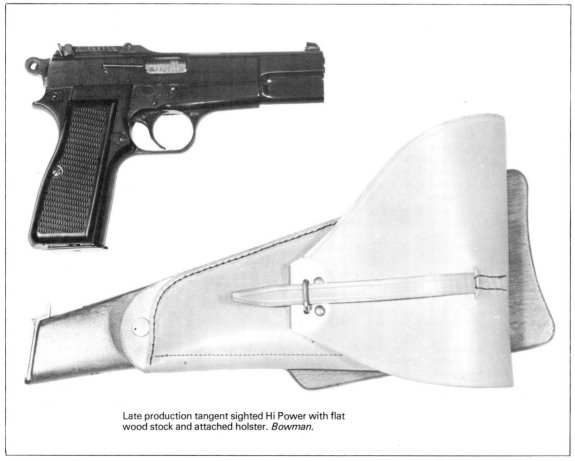

Late production tangent sighted Hi Power with flat wood stock and attached holster. *Bowman.*

Inglis Browning

During World War II the Browning was manufactured in Canada by John Inglis Co Ltd of Toronto. These weapons were produced, not only for supply under Lease-Lend to the British, but also for Canada's own forces and for the Greek and Chinese National Armies. Mr Baldwin, the Assistant Secretary of John Inglis, told the author the

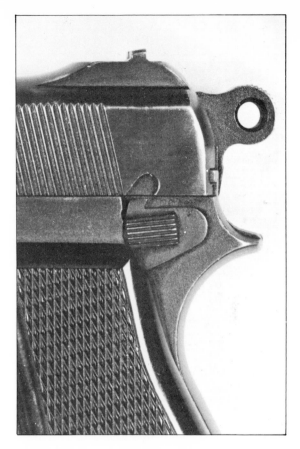

Inglis Browning fixed rear and front sight No. 2 Mark 1 (*Pattern Room, Enfield*)

Inglis Browning Mark 1 * (*Pattern Room, Enfield*)

Below: Detail of mark number

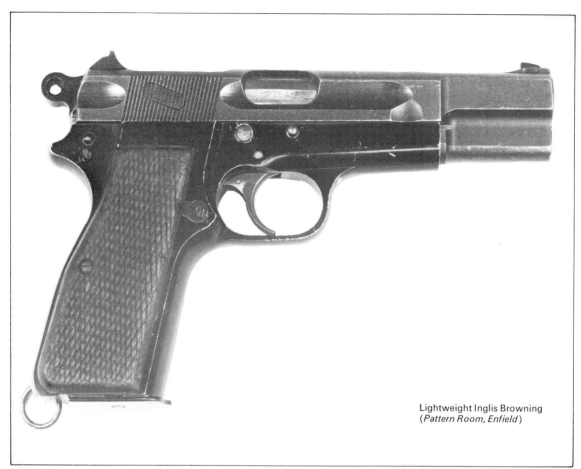

Lightweight Inglis Browning
(*Pattern Room, Enfield*)

following interesting story. After Inglis had undertaken to manufacture the pistol, the Government were unable to obtain delivery of the drawings necessary for production, which were somewhere in the south of France. As an alternative the Government obtained six hand-fitted pistols manufactured by Fabrique Nationale from an undisclosed source. John Inglis then, from these hand-fitted samples, made their own component drawings and established dimensions and tolerances, so as to ensure complete interchangeability of parts. When the Belgian drawings were obtained, at a later date, John Inglis were most surprised to find that they were almost exactly the same.

The pistol was produced in two versions, one for the British which had fixed sights and one with an elevated back sight, some of which had wooden shoulder stock holsters which were supplied to the

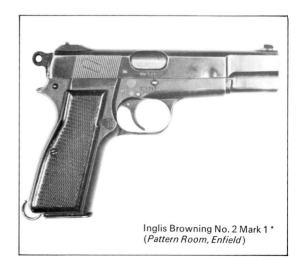

Inglis Browning No. 2 Mark 1 *
(*Pattern Room, Enfield*)

Chinese Nationalists. During the war, starting in 1943, Inglis turned out 151,800 Browning pistols. The Inglis Browning, now, is standard issue in the British Army along with Browning's Hi-Power produced by F.N.

Inglis modified the pistols as follows : No. 1 Mark 1, a shoulder stock fitted with adjustable tangent sights. No. 1 Mark 1*, was also fitted with shoulder stock, but a modified extractor required the changing of the tangent sight position—the extractor is not interchangeable with that of the earlier weapon. No. 2 Mark 1, was a pistol without shoulder stock fixed sights and the Mark 1 extractor system. No. 2 Mark 1*, a similar pistol to the No. 2 Mark 1 using the latter extractor and ejector. Inglis also produced a lightweight version of the Hi-Power but this was only experimental and was never introduced as tests indicated that after 2000 rounds the alloy frame began to fret.

An interesting note on the reliability of the Browning was a test given to it by the Canadian Government before adoption. This was a sand box into which ammunition and the parts of two guns were dumped. The mixture was well stirred and then the two guns were reassembled, slides locked back and the guns loaded. Once again more sand was added. The guns only required a shake to clear the surplus sand and although a little rough in action, both weapons fired with no stoppages.

Browning (Detail) Lightening cut outs
(*Pattern Room, Enfield*)

Brigadier

The North American Arms Corporation of Canada produced a modified Hi-Power called the Brigadier. This weapon was designed to fire a super ·45 automatic pistol cartridge which had a 230 grain bullet, attaining a velocity of 1600fps. The Brigadier, of which possibly only one or two prototypes were made, had a light alloy receiver, a removable hammer and trigger group (similar to the Russian Tokarev) and a double action trigger. The

dimensions are : 9·62in. long, 5·5in. barrel, weight 4·18lb with a magazine capacity of 8 cartridges.

It will have been noticed from previous remarks made that a large number of engraved weapons have been manufactured by F.N. This is explained by the fact that F.N. has some 150 engravers on its payroll. It is probably the largest single group of engravers in the world. F.N. have always specialised in this extra finish.

Exploded view Browning Hi-Power   (*FN*)

BROWNING AUTOMATIC PISTOLS SPECIFICATIONS

Model	Length	Height	Barrel length	Calibre	Mag. cap.	Weight
1900	6·75″	4·75″	4″	·32ACP	7	22oz
1903	8″	116mm	5″	9mmBL	7	32oz
	205mm		128mm			930g
Mod. 10 ·32ACP	6″	4″	3·5″	·32ACP	7	20·5oz
Mod. 10 ·380ACP	6″	4″	3·5″	·380ACP	6	20oz
10/22 ·32ACP	7″	4·75″	4·5″	·32ACP	9	25oz
10/22 ·380ACP	7″	4·75″	4·5″	·380ACP	8	24oz
1935 Hi-Power	8″	5″	4·75″	9mm PAR	13	32oz
First Model 1906 ·25	5″	2·875″	2·5″	·25ACP	6	13·5oz
Baby	4″	2·875″	2·1″	·25ACP	6	9·5oz
	104mm	72mm				275g
Lightweight Baby	4″	2·875″	2·1″	·25ACP	6	7·75oz
	104mm	72mm				
Brigadier	9·62″	N.A.	5·5″	·45NAAC Special	8	4·18lb

Browning NAAC Brigadier

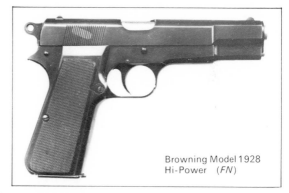

Browning Model 1928
Hi-Power   (*FN*)

Partially machined components for Browning Hi-Power (*FN*)

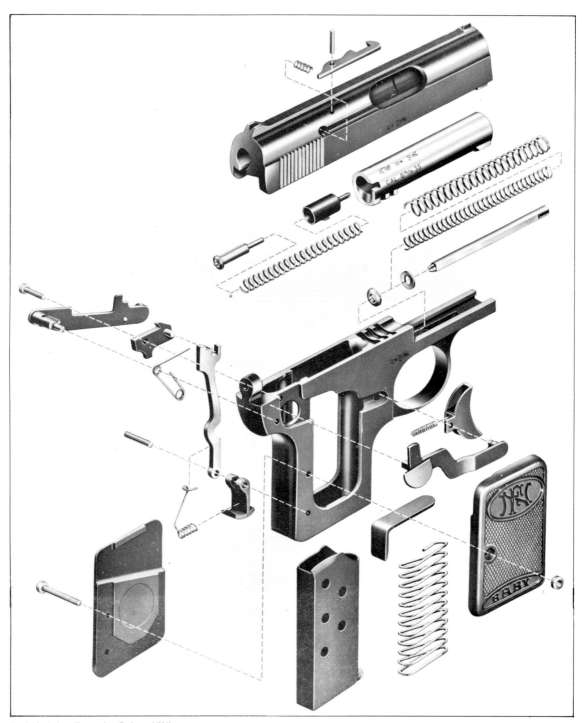

Exploded view Browning Baby   (*FN*)

Webley 9mm Parabellum Experimental Model
(*Pattern Room, Enfield*)

Webley and Scott Automatic Pistols

A. J. R. Cormack

An expert can often tell the origin of a pistol by its look and finish. One would not need to be an expert to identify the Webley automatic pistol. The unmistakable square features could only come from the country from which emanates the bulldog breed. This is a weapon which has no pretensions to beauty but has an honest look of reliable dependability. The idea behind and the development of the Webley automatic pistol took place in four stages. First, the ill-fated Mars Fairfax pistol which, although of a most advanced design, never achieved commercial success. (The failure of the Mars set Mr Webley the task of developing a reliable and commercially viable automatic pistol.) Second, the successful range of automatic pistols developed and put into production, between 1903 and 1940. Third, the Harrington and Richardson Licence Built pistols, and fourth, the 9mm parabellum pistol developed unsuccessfully for small arms trials around 1952.

(The failure of this pistol probably stopped any chance of the British small arms industry equipping any future British Armed Forces with an automatic pistol.)

Mars Pistol

This weapon will be dealt with in a future Profile, however a short description is necessary to understand the development of the Webley range. The Mars is a massive strong locked breech pistol. It fires a number of different bottle necked cartridges. Considering the date of its design and production, which was between 1895 and 1907, the power achieved by the ammunition and weapon can only be considered astounding. However, this massive construction, so necessary with such high powered cartridges and the complication of the basic mechanism, led to its non-acceptance.

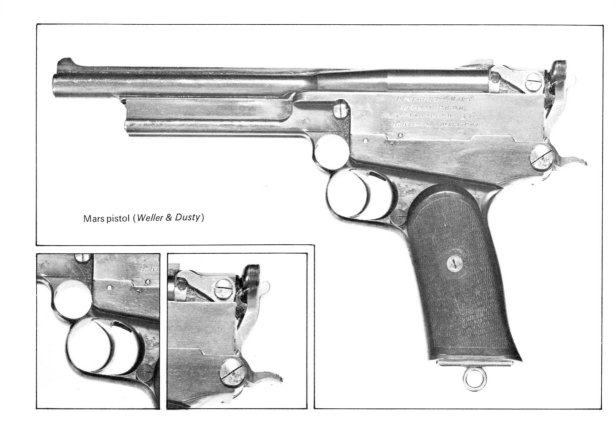

Mars pistol (*Weller & Dusty*)

Webley Automatics
·455 Experimental Automatic

1903 Prototype: The 1903 prototype was developed under the guidance of Mr Whiting who was under the direct control of Mr T. W. Webley. This pistol was patented on 4 September 1902 (Patent No. 19032). The weapon was designed to chamber the ·455 rimmed revolver cartridge and not the later ·455 Webley automatic cartridge. An external hammer was used as in all future ·455 automatics. The locking system was interesting in that the locking was accomplished by two pivoted locking pieces mounted externally on the slide which were held by cams into engagement with recesses in the barrel. On recoil different cams pushed the locking levers out of engagement allowing the breech to open. A recoil spring closed the breech chambering a new round.

Webley ·455 Experimental Automatic 1903

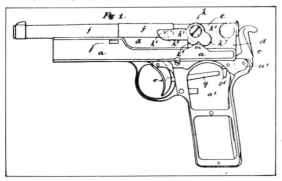

1904 Prototype: In 1904 a patent was taken out (No. 3820) on 16 February, followed by further patents in August and November of the same year, for a new type of locking system. This weapon far from being a simplified one, was most complicated in design and construction. The locking system involved a vertical sliding bolt and a barrel latch which combined to give a not very reliable operation. The patent in August (No. 17856), was for a hold-open device and the November patent contained further details of this device, also details of a stripping device and a trigger mechanism to prevent double shots. This weapon was chambered for a modified cartridge with first the regulation rim plus a groove and finally the semi-rimmed type used in the later pistols. The 'V' recoil spring was adopted and continued throughout most of the Webley designs. This weapon was tested by the British Government in October 1904 and also in March 1905. The results would seem to be somewhat contradictory as on one test the weapon was found satisfactory and on another completely unsatisfactory. The weapon was $10\frac{1}{4}$in. long, weighed 3lb $1\frac{1}{4}$oz and had a barrel length of $6\frac{1}{2}$in. The magazine carried 7 rounds.

1906 Prototype: A further design, a stage nearer the final one, was patented on 13 June 1906 (No. 13570). This model was the first to use the inclined rib type of lock. The basic mechanism works as follows:
The barrel is free to slide in three ribs on either side of the main body, these ribs are inclined forward at an angle of 45°. When the slide closes under the influence of the 'V' recoil spring the barrel is forced

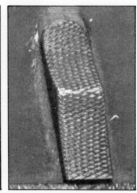

Webley ·455 Experimental
Automatic 1904
(*Pattern Room, Enfield*)

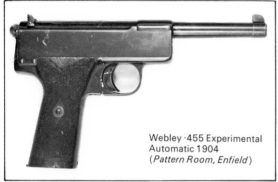
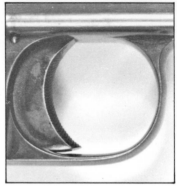

Webley ·455 Experimental
Automatic 1904
(*Pattern Room, Enfield*)

forwards and upwards guided by these ribs. As it moves upwards a rib on the top engages with a corresponding rib on the slide, thereby locking the slide and barrel together. When the weapon is fired the fact that the slots are at an angle coupled with the help of the friction of the inclined surfaces holds the slide and barrel together until the pressure drops sufficiently to allow safe ejection. When the pressure has dropped to a safe limit the barrel moves rearward and downward allowing the slide to move backward ejecting the empty case. The weapon was tested by the British Army and progressive modifications made. A report in September 1909 indicates modifications to the safety and to the trigger, and in October 1909, 1254 rounds were fired with only one failure. This was combined with an accuracy rated

higher than that of the issue Service Revolver. In September 1910 in competition with the Colt model 1905 ·45 automatic (described in the *Profile* No. 5 'The Colt ·45 Automatic') the report favoured the Webley and found the Colt unsafe. The conclusion of the tests suggested that modifications to the safety were necessary and that the Army required a lighter pistol.

Model 1912 ·455 Mk. I

This weapon was the one finally adopted for Government Service. The Royal Navy accepted it as a limited standard weapon on 19 May 1914. It was also used by the Royal Marines. The basic differences between this weapon and the 1906 concerned those enumerated above, plus the fitting

Webley ·455 Locking system
(*Lowland Brigade Depot*)

Webley ·455 Mk. I Model 1912
(*Bowman*)

Webley ·455 Mk. I Demonstration Model
(*Pattern Room, Enfield*)

of a grip safety and the reduction of the ribs from six to four—albeit larger ones—thus simplifying machining. The magazine release was standardised as the button type used on all later pistols and the dismounting pin modified for ease of use. This weapon was also produced for commercial sale and one such ·455 automatic was used by the Vauxhall Factory Guards during the Second World War by which time the Webley was not a front line service weapon although it would still act as a powerful deterrent to an intruder.

·455 Mk. I No. 2

Records would indicate that 100 Webley ·455's were issued to the Royal Horse Artillery in 1913,

—50 of which had shoulder stocks—and to the Royal Flying Corps on 26 April 1915. The Model 1915 differs little from the 1912 except that it has an additional safety and a new type of back sight similar to the one fitted to the Luger which adjusts automatically for windage. Keeping in mind the similarity, it would seem that the progression from 1912 to 1915 is far from distinct. One interesting feature was that the magazine had a second holding notch whereby it could be held only partly in, thus allowing the pistol to be loaded single shot fashion keeping the full magazine in reserve. The advantages of this system rather escape the author but they are possibly explained by a paragraph in the Manual of Military Engineering dated 1893 which although referring to the magazine fed Lee-Metford would

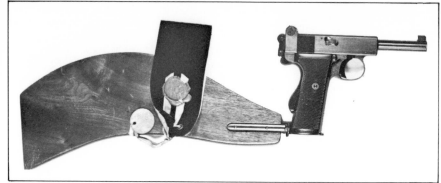

Webley ·455 Mk. I No. 2. *Note:* The Pattern Room Seal of acceptance. This indicates that the weapon has been accepted as suitable for production *(Pattern Room, Enfield)*

Webley ·455 Mk. I No. 2
Note Safety catch
(Pattern Room, Enfield)

seem appropriate—'As a single loader (it) will fire about 12 aimed shots a minute. *The magazine is kept as a reserve for critical moments.'*

·38 ACP Model 1904

This weapon was the first attempt by Webley to manufacture a ·38/9mm. calibre pistol and naturally enough the 1904 ·455 automatic was used as a basis. The weapon is chambered for the ·38 ACP cartridge and as can be seen is identical in all major features to its larger brother. The lock system employed is also basically the same as the ·455. Only a very few of these weapons have survived and it may be assumed that as the highest numbered one known is No. 29 the weapon never attained production quantity. The reason for this could be the lack of interest at the turn of the century in a small calibre weapon. The calibre used by all major countries was ·45 or larger.

·38 High Velocity Hammerless Automatic Models 1910 & 1913

With the possible changing of military requirement from a weapon firing the low velocity large bore ·455 revolver or automatic cartridge, to that of a smaller bore high velocity cartridge, Webley decided to develop a weapon suitable for the latter. The cartridge chosen was the ·38 ACP which had

received acceptance with the line of Colt automatic pistols. The model 1909 9mm which had been chambered for the 9mm Browning Long Cartridge was a simple blow-back weapon and therefore not suitable for the use of a high velocity cartridge. As there was already in existence at this time the ·455 automatic which was chambered for the relatively powerful ·455 automatic round and thus had a locked breech, it was logical that the ·38 ACP weapon should be a modified version of this.
The first version is normally identified as the Model 1910 and the only basic difference between it and the ·455 Mk. I is that an internal hammer is used. It has a barrel length of 5in. and a magazine capacity of eight. In 1913 the modified version 'the Model 1913' was developed. The major change being the adoption of a safety catch similar to that on the ·32 automatic. These weapons are, with the exception

Webley ·38 ACP Model 1904
Note: Similarity to ·455 Model 1904 *(Frame)*

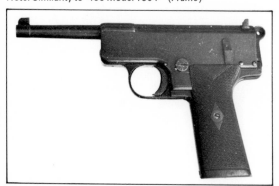

Webley ·38 High Velocity Model
(Imperial War Museum)

Webley ·38 High Velocity Model
(Pattern Room, Enfield)

of the 9mm parabellum automatics, the rarest of all Webley automatic pistols.

9mm Browning Long, External Hammer Automatic Model 1909

This pistol was developed after Webley & Scott had, along with various other American and Continental manufacturers, submitted for trial a number of pistols to European Governments. The outcome of these tests was that although the weapons concerned (probably calibres ·32 or ·455) met with approval by these Governments, the calibres for which they were chambered did not. As a result Webley decided to manufacture a pistol with a calibre of 9mm. It was chosen because the 9mm Browning Long was a popular pistol and sub machine gun cartridge much used in Europe at the time. It had also the advantage of being sufficiently

Police Force in 1920 as their official automatic pistol. The main patent numbers 1664; 2569; 19177 were taken out in 1908.

One of the interesting features of the weapon is that the grip safety and the trigger mechanism are manufactured as a single unit and thus the sear is held away from the trigger bar until the grip safety along with the trigger mechanism is pressed into a position where they can make contact. The weapon continues with the method adopted in the ·32 automatic of holding the barrel to the receiver by the trigger guard. Unlike the other weapons ·25 ACP, ·32 ACP, ·380 ACP, there is a positive hold-open device fitted. This differs from the other weapons in that the slide stays back when the last round has been fired and is held there by the magazine follower. Needless to say on the extraction of the magazine the slide returns forward. On the 9mm however, the slide has a positive hold-open and for it

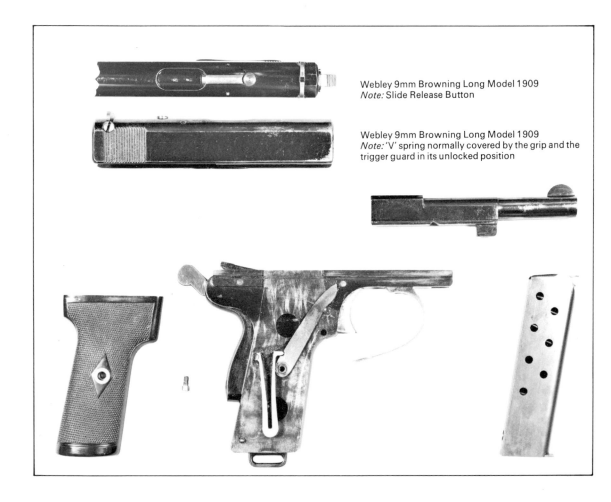

Webley 9mm Browning Long Model 1909
Note: Slide Release Button

Webley 9mm Browning Long Model 1909
Note: 'V' spring normally covered by the grip and the trigger guard in its unlocked position

low pressured to enable a blow back design to be adopted. A large number of patents were taken out during the development of this weapon, between 1908 and 1909. Webley manufactured some 20 weapons by hand for further trials before the commencement of production in 1909. This pistol was eventually adopted by the South African

to be closed the small button on the top of the slide has to be depressed.

Some of the earlier weapons were produced with a safety catch on the right hand side but on all later weapons it was of a similar type to the later ·32. Two types of grips were employed, one of hard rubber and the other of bakelite.

Webley 9mm Browning
Long Model 1909
Note: Retailers' name engraved on the slide
(*Pattern Room, Enfield*)

Note: Grip safety in its
locked position

This weapon was also tested by the British Government who although it had found acceptance by the others, described it has having a number of faults and, in any case, not conforming to the required specification.

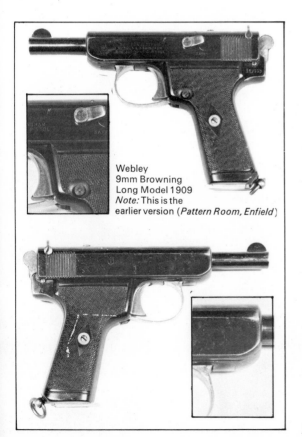

Webley
9mm Browning
Long Model 1909
Note: This is the
earlier version (*Pattern Room, Enfield*)

·380 Automatic Model 1905

This weapon is identical to the ·32 1905 and its construction is covered by the patents applying to that weapon, therefore no separate description of it is necessary.

·32 ACP External Hammer Model 1905

This weapon was designed by W. J. Whiting and patented in 1904 (Patent No. 15982). It was first marketed in 1905 and continued in a series of modified forms to be produced until 1940. It is, therefore, the Webley automatic which attained the largest acceptance and production volume. It went through three basic phases of design, starting with the 1905 production model which has a fixed barrel and the simple blow back design of the later models. The distinguishing features of the 1905 are the external trigger bar, the thick trigger, the multi-ring hammer and the safety catch which is mounted on the left hand side of the hammer.

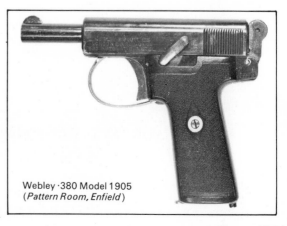

Webley ·380 Model 1905
(*Pattern Room, Enfield*)

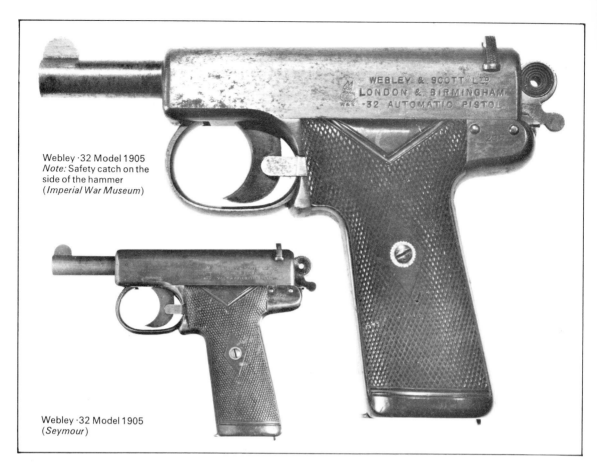

Webley ·32 Model 1905
Note: Safety catch on the side of the hammer
(*Imperial War Museum*)

Webley ·32 Model 1905
(*Seymour*)

1906 Model

Model 1906 had a modified safety covered by Patent No. 24382 1 November 1906. This modification moved the safety from the side of the hammer to a position on the top of the left grip. The movement was now in a vertical plane. One interim version is illustrated in the Webley Catalogue of the time and shows a weapon with the early type of hammer, early trigger guard and external trigger bar, but with a safety of the later type. It must be remembered that Webley throughout the production of this weapon employed a policy of continual improvement and as a result some interim weapons cannot be classified into the normally accepted divisions.

Model 1913

A number of different patents were taken out for modifications before the final 1913 version, the main one being No. 2468 dated 30 January 1913. The main differences in the Model 1913 are the replacement of the external trigger bar by an internal one, the use of a hammer without the tings and the

Webley ·32 Model 1913
Note: Imperial Airways Ltd Stamp   (*Smart*)

Webley ·32 Model 1906
(*Seymour*)

Webley ·32 Model 1913

Webley ·32 Model 1913

safety operating in the radial manner at the top of the left hand grip. There were two main versions of the 1913 model, the first produced for the Police. This weapon was adopted in 1911 by the London and Metropolitan Forces and then by numerous other Police Forces throughout Britain. It is interesting that the reason for the adoption by the Police of a fire-arm was as a result of the famous or infamous Battle of Sidney Street which, under the direction of the then Home Secretary Winston Churchill, resulted in troops being called after two Policemen had been murdered. The 1913 Police Model is identified by the later 'thin' trigger guard, the radial safety and normally an adjustable backsight. The second version was the Civilian equivalent of

Webley ·32 Model 1913
Note: Metropolitan Police stamp and Lanyard Loop fitted to some Police Weapons
(*Lowland Brigade Depot*)

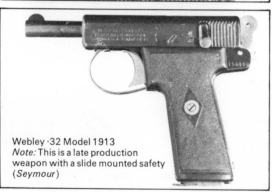

Webley ·32 Model 1913
Note: This is a late production weapon with a slide mounted safety
(*Seymour*)

the above. The only difference in specification was in most cases the deletion of the adjustable sight and the substitution of a machined groove in the slide to act as a sight. A further variant illustrated shows a change to slide mounted safety catch. This is a late production weapon.

One interesting weapon illustrated is a ·32 ACP automatic marked 'Imperial Airways'. A former

Webley ·32 Model 1913
An adaptation of the basic weapon for use as a Humane Killer
(*Pattern Room, Enfield*)

Captain in Imperial Airways related that along with Beau Geste Forts and machine guns near Sharja on the Omar Peninsula where there would be some danger, Imperial Airways issued this weapon. This can only make the present situation of hi-jacked airliners and the controversies regarding armed guards a case of history repeating itself.

An early catalogue for the ·32 Webley automatic pistol sums up many of the intentions of the Webley Company. It names strength, simplicity of construction, small bulk and light weight as the pistol's greatest assets, and goes on to say that the Webley automatic pistol has amongst other advantages over the common revolver the following: ease of manipulation, rapidity of fire, accuracy of aim, increased velocity and penetration. It further remarks that owing to the construction, the recoil is largely absorbed by the moving parts thus leading to greater accuracy on the second shot.

·25 External Hammer Experimental Model 1906

The initial ·25 Webley which was not developed and bore no relation to the later weapons in this calibre was patented by Mr J. Carter on 22 December 1906 (Patent No. 29221). The reason that Mr Carter patented this weapon, rather than its designer Mr W. J. Whiting, was that the latter was on a tour of the United States. Mr W. J. Whiting was probably the foremost handgun designer in Britain at this time. The trip to the United States, by Mr Whiting, probably resulted in the Harrington & Richardson Arms Co. manufacturing under licence the later model ·25 and ·32 weapons. These will be described under a separate heading. The 1906 ·25, unlike most weapons developed in the Webley family, uses a single coil spring as the recoil spring. It was a simple blowback weapon, as were all Webley automatic pistols, with the exception of the ·38 ACP, 9mm parabellum and ·455.

Webley ·25 Model 1906/1940
Note: Retailers' name engraved on the slide
(*Pattern Room, Enfield*)

Webley ·25 Model 1906/1940
(*Pattern Room, Enfield*)

Webley ·32 Model 1913
Note: Machine groove acting as a sight

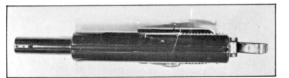

1906/1940 Model

For one reason or another, probably that of simplicity, it was decided to develop the ·25 ACP automatic on the lines of the 1906 ·32 ACP weapon. The designs of the ·25 ACP, ·32 ACP and ·380 ACP blowback automatics are so similar that Webley uses one diagram to illustrate the parts for all three weapons.

Webley ·25 Model 1904
(*Pattern Room, Enfield*)

·25 ACP Hammerless Model 1909

This weapon, covered by Patent Nos. 23564 15 October 1909 and No. 20367 1 September 1910, is the smallest and simplest of all Webley automatic pistols. It has only four main parts, the body, barrel, breech slide and magazine. Although it is similar to the previously described ·25 ACP pistols in that it is a straight blowback, it does however have the V spring replaced with twin coil springs. These springs are mounted on either side of the firing pin in the slide. The ·25 ACP is often known, as the heading indicates, as a hammerless pistol but this is not its true designation as it has a concealed hammer.

Below right: Webley ·22 Model 1911 Long Barrel
Note: Different construction from that of the ·32 (1913)
(*Pattern Room, Enfield*)
Below: Webley ·22 Model 1911 Long Barrel   (*Bowman*)

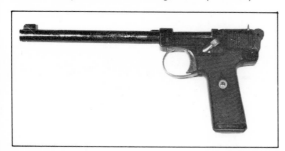

Webley ·32 Harrington & Richardson
(*Dalgleish*)

Webley ·32 Harrington & Richardson
(*Pattern Room, Enfield*)

Webley ·25
Harrington & Richardson
(*Pattern Room, Enfield*)

Webley ·25
Harrington & Richardson
(*Pattern Room, Enfield*)

The 1911 ·22 Single Shot Semi-Automatic Pistol

This weapon which was used by the Metropolitan and other Police Forces in a 4½in. barrel version for practice was based on the issue ·32 ACP automatic. This meant that men could be trained with a weapon that was identical in handling to that of the official issue. A model with a 9in. barrel along with a shoulder stock was also available. The weapon is an oddity to say the least in that although the slide is blown back on firing and ejects the empty case, it remains open and the pistol has to be manually loaded with a single round and the slide closed again. In other words it is more an automatic ejector than a semi-automatic pistol. A hand ejector is also fitted for use in the event that the spent case is not blown clear.

Harrington & Richardson Arms Co. ·25 and ·32 Automatic Pistols

The above weapons were covered under Webley's American patents in August 1907 and April 1909. These patents were assigned by Webley & Co. to the Harrington & Richardson Arms Co. The ·25 ACP was introduced in 1912 and remained in production for a period of three years, about 20,000 being manufactured. In 1916 H & R introduced the ·32 ACP which was a modification of the basic Webley design in that it was a striker fired weapon as opposed to the Webley concealed hammer or hammers. Production of this pistol ceased in 1939.

The basic difference other than that mentioned between these pistols and their corresponding Webley counterparts was the use of a coil recoil spring as opposed to the 'V' type.

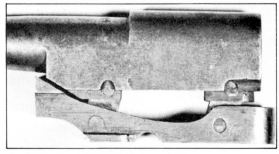

Jurek. The Twin Link locking system and its Cradle
(*Dr. Jurek*)

9mm Parabellum Prototype Automatics

The result of the trials for which Webley had submitted an entry was that the Browning Hi-Power was chosen. The Webley entrant is however of great interest both historically and technically. The designer, Dr Marian K. Jurek, was born in Poland on 7 September 1904 and even at the age of 15 was dabbling in the art of the gunmaker. In 1937, after a brilliant scholastic career, Dr Jurek became the Head of Research at an ammunition factory. During the war Dr Jurek saw service with a number of branches of the Services including the 1st Armoured Division Workshops. In 1946, while still a serving member of the Parachute Regiment, he designed two submachine guns which fired from a closed bolt and used a separate hammer to reduce

Jurek 9mm Parabellum Prototype
Note: Progressive increase in the number of locking lugs
(*Dr Jurek*)

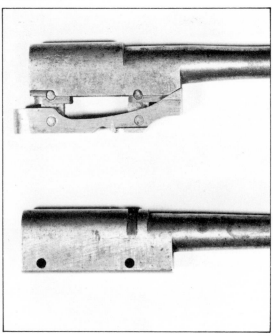

Webley 9mm Parabellum Prototype
Note: Progressive increase in the number of locking lugs
(*Webley & Scott*)

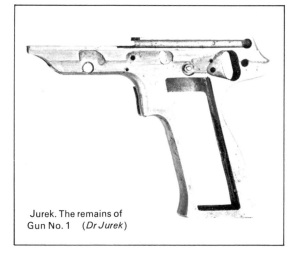

Jurek. The remains of
Gun No. 1 (*Dr Jurek*)

the rate of fire. Also of note was the small diameter recoil spring mounted on a removable guide rod. This rod ran through the breech block giving a simple and reliable operation. Both weapons were demonstrated to the BAOR and later in Britain, but were rejected by a Board which Dr Jurek asserted did not give the weapons a fair trial. Dr Jurek believes that one of these weapons would have been a suitable replacement for the Sten, both on grounds of reliability and cost.

After the lack of success with the submachine guns, Dr Jurek in December 1946, designed and made from mild steel an automatic pistol. Although only the receiver remains, it is evident that the design features remained constant throughout the range of pistols. The basic difference between the locking on the Jurek pistol and that of the Colt/Browning range is that although the locking ribs on the barrel and slide are similar, the movement of the barrel is controlled by a parallel twin link system. These links are attached to a separate cradle which, with the action of the links and a close fit with the barrel on lock up, ensure that the barrel returns to exactly the same position for each shot. This offers considerable advantages and enables the pistol in all of its forms to shoot with superb accuracy.

In September 1949 Dr Jurek joined Webley but it

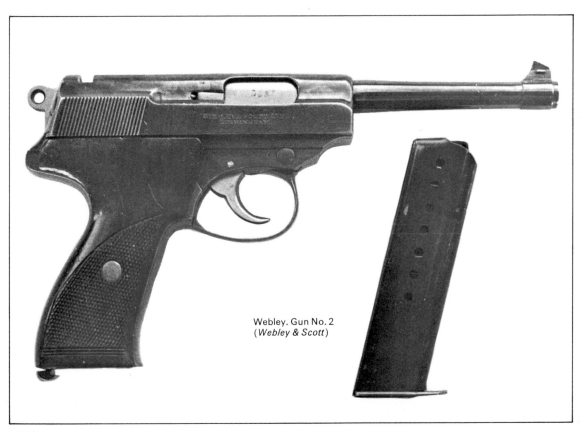

Webley. Gun No. 2
(*Webley & Scott*)

Webley. Gun No. 2
(*Webley & Scott*)

Jurek. Working drawing for Gun No. 4   (*Dr Jurek*)

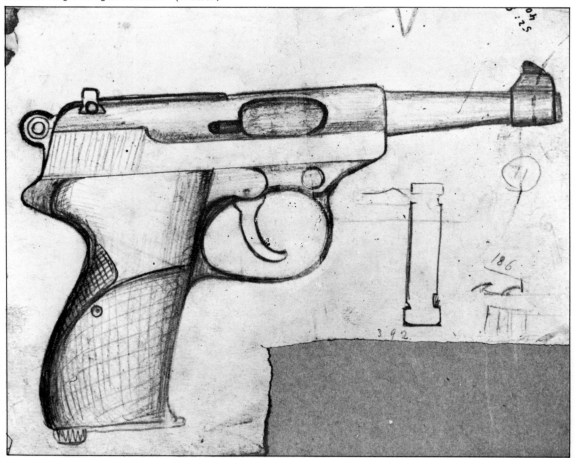

was not until 1952, when Webley decided to submit a pistol for test by the Government, that he redesigned his pistol and manufactured a prototype in an extremely short space of time. This weapon is Pistol No. 2 or Webley No. 1.

The results of the test indicate that the Board would like the weapon to be made lighter possibly with the use of an alloy receiver, a better pull on the double action trigger and improved sealing against dirt. Two further requests were that a magazine safety be incorporated and a ·22 training weapon be manufactured. Dr Jurek agreed that these requests were all possible. As a result of the tests Dr Jurek made in only a few weeks a third pistol (Webley No. 2). The resulting weapon was tested and although much improved it was not yet judged entirely satisfactory. The use of an alloy receiver was recommended so that a side-by-side test could be arranged with one having a steel receiver. It is noteworthy that this recommendation was after a report that the experimental alloy frame Browning Hi-Power had developed signs of fretting after only 2000 rounds. Dr Jurek asserts, however, that with the separate cradle design the fretting problem would not have been encountered. A desire was also

expressed for a 13 round magazine, this being obviously in comparison with the Browning Hi-Power. See Small Arms *Profile* No. 2.

Although there was a request for a further model coupled with the alloy framed weapon and a ·22 training weapon development was suspended suddenly by Webley. This can only be attributed to the fact that the Browning had been accepted. The only fault of a major nature which had been found during testing was that a slight bulging of the slide was encountered. This had been easily remedied.

After the cessation of work on this and other pistols Dr Jurek left Webley and started up a small gun repair shop with enough machines to continue producing a range of target pistols. These pistols all exhibit superb workmanship and an appreciation of the needs of the target shot which could only be understood by a person with international qualifications for that sport.

The final chapter cannot be written because it is only a drawing and an image of the fertile imagination of Dr Jurek. The weapon which emerges will have a number of detailed modifications to make it perhaps the best automatic pistol ever produced.

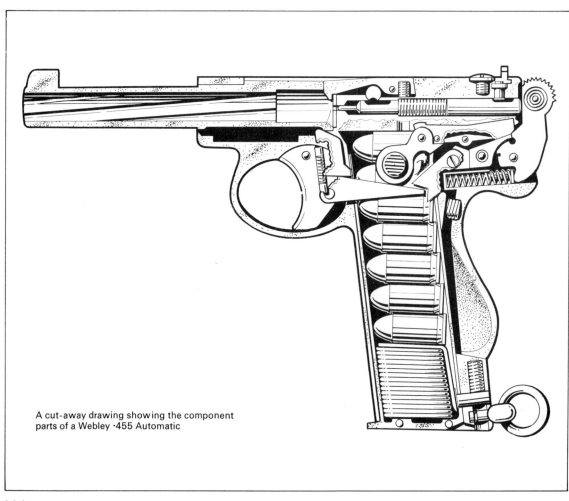

A cut-away drawing showing the component parts of a Webley ·455 Automatic

WEBLEY AUTOMATIC PISTOLS SPECIFICATION

Model	Length	Height	Barrel length	Calibre	Mag. cap.	Weight
·22 Single Shot	6·5"/11"	4·5"	4·5"/9"	·22 L.R.	none	22/23¾oz
·25 Experimental	4·75"	3·125"	—	·25 ACP	6	—
·25 External Hammer	4·75"	3·125"	2·125"	·25 ACP	6	11¾oz
·25 Internal Hammer	4·25"	3·125"	2·125"	·25 ACP	6	10¼oz
·32 1905-1913	6·25"	4·5"	3·5"	·32 ACP	8	20oz
·38 1904 High Velocity	10"	—	6·5"	·38 ACP	9	2lb 8½oz
·38 High Velocity	8"	5·5"	5"	·38 ACP	8	—
9mm Browning Long	8"	5"	5·5"	9mm Browning Long	8	34oz
9mm Parabellum	9·5"	5·5"	4"/6"	9mm Parabellum	8	—
·455 Experimental	10"	6"	—	·455	7	—
·455 Production	8·5"	5·5"	5"	·455	7	39oz
·25 Harrington & Richardson	4·5"	3⅛"	2⅛"	·25 ACP	6	12½oz
·32 Harrington & Richardson	6·5"	—	3·5"	·32 ACP	8	20oz

Webley. Gun No. 3
(*Pattern Room, Enfield*)

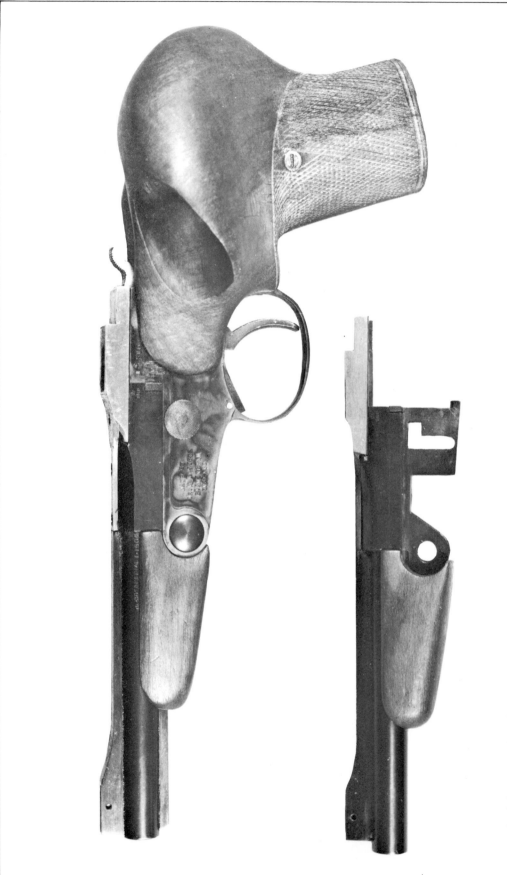

Jurek Convertible ·22/·38 Target Pistol. This is not an automatic pistol, but included to show the excellence of his work (*Dr Jurek*)

Beretta Model 1915 calibre
7·65mm. Notice the safety lever
(*US Army Infantry Museum,
Ft. Benning*)

The Beretta

by A. J. R. Cormack

Formed before 1680, the firm of Beretta has a history that follows closely the development of the pistol from its beginnings. A family firm which has always been and still is in the Beretta family, it continues to reflect in the mass-production age the pride of craftsmanship which was lavished on the first hand-made weapons.

From a notebook dated 1732 which is now in the Beretta archives, it can be established that the firm as such was originally founded in 1680. However, as the Valley of Trompia, where Beretta was established, had been a centre for arms makers much earlier it is more than possible that the forefathers of the founder Pietro Beretta had been engaged in the trade. As early as 1420 the tradesmen of the area had united into a guild to manufacture muzzle-loading weapons. The forge used by the Beretta family had a door lintel dated 1500 which would indicate that the family was in the trade from the

start. This lintel is now incorporated in the present factory building as part of the tradition handed down.

Pietro Beretta de Lodovico at the age of 30, founded a barrel shop in 1680 following his family's long association with firearms and specifically with forging. The one fact above all which made the continuance of the family concern possible was that each of the marriages during the early years turned out to be blessed with large numbers of children. Pietro Beretta was succeeded by the eldest of his eight sons, Pier Guiseppe, who in turn had nine children, all of whom worked in the firm. Pier Antonio Lodovico, born in 1729 the eldest of Pier Guiseppe's nine children assumed command and in turn produced eight children, the eldest of whom—Pier Guiseppe Antonio, took over the firm on his father's death.

In succession there followed Pier Antonio, a further

117

Beretta Flintlock pistol dating from 1700. (*Beretta*)

Pier Guiseppe Antonio, Pietro and finally the present Chairman Pier Guiseppe and his brother Pier Carlo his assistant. Under these energetic leaders the factory grew and in 1880 the first of the modern production plants was set up. The number of employees also mounted from 118 in 1903, to 300 in 1918 and today to 1600. The present factory, which produces every part of the weapons including bolts, springs, woodwork and barrels, now covers 49000 square metres and uses some fifteen tons of iron and six tons of wood per year. Because Beretta produce every part of their weapons the quality which was evident in the early days can be retained today and assured in the future.

Model 1915

The Model 1915 was manufactured in two calibres; the popular ·32ACP (7·65mm) and the ineffective 9mm Glisenti (M10 Glisenti). The 9mm Glisenti is a low powered cartridge with the same dimensions as 9mm parabellum but being less powerful makes a straight blowback operated pistol such as the Model 1915 possible. Of great importance is a warning that if a 9mm parabellum round is fired in this or any weapon chambered for the 9mm Glisenti there is a great danger of damage to the weapon and the firer.

The 7·65 Model 1915 is a straight blowback pistol with few identifiable features. The ejection port is on the top of the slide near the muzzle, a feature that was to be retained on many later weapons. The safety catch is on the left side and doubles as a slide catch. As there is no separate ejector the firing pin therefore acts as one. The sights are fixed and on some weapons there is a lanyard loop on the left of the butt. The magazine catch is on the base of the butt and the magazine contains seven rounds. As mentioned above, the 9mm Glisenti Model 1915 is a blowback operated weapon being very similar to the ·32ACP (7·65mm) 1915 but longer overall and having a recoil buffer fitted to supplement the recoil spring. The safety catch and magazine catch are the same as the ·32ACP version but the magazine contains eight rounds.

On the 9mm Model 1915 the magazine follower acts as a slide hold open and unlike the ·32ACP version there is an ejector.

This weapon was issued to the police as well as being a standard sidearm for the Regio Esercito (The Royal Army). It did not remain in production after 1919.

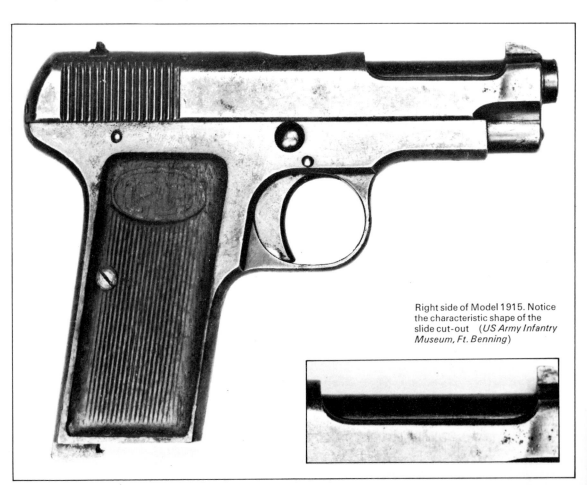

Right side of Model 1915. Notice the characteristic shape of the slide cut-out (*US Army Infantry Museum, Ft. Benning*)

Right side of 7·65mm Model 1915. Notice the 'Not English Made' stamp showing that this weapon was imported to Britain   (*Pattern Room Enfield*)

A Beretta Model 1915 chambered for 9mm short (·380ACP)

Right side of 9mm short Model 1915
(*Pattern Room, Enfield*)

Left side of Model 1915/1919 showing the safety catch in both safe and fire positions

(Pattern Room, Enfield)   *(Dalgleish)*

Right side of Model 1915/19 showing the characteristic PB emblem and the butt extension fitted to the magazine
(Pattern Room, Enfield)

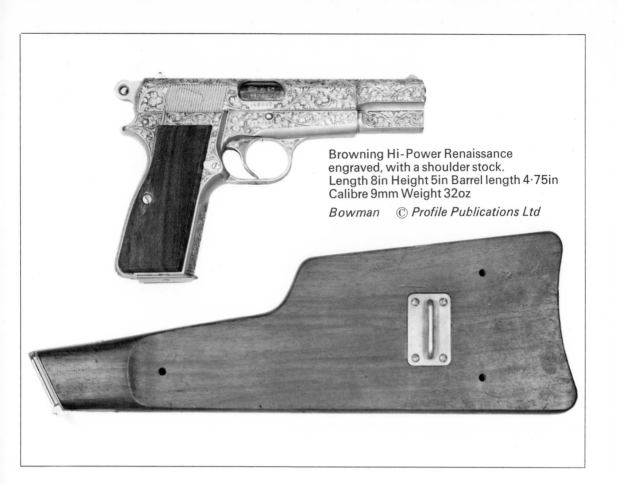

Browning Hi-Power Renaissance
engraved, with a shoulder stock.
Length 8in Height 5in Barrel length 4·75in
Calibre 9mm Weight 32oz

Bowman © *Profile Publications Ltd*

A standard Browning Hi-Power or P.35.
This weapon has a tangent rear sight.
Length 8in Height 5in Barrel length 4·75in
Calibre 9mm Weight 32oz

Bowman © *Profile Publications Ltd*

Browning Hi-Power with the factory Renaissance engraving.
This finish is still available from Fabrique National.
Length 8in Height 5in Barrel length 4·75in Calibre 9mm
Weight 32oz

Bowman © *Profile Publications Ltd*

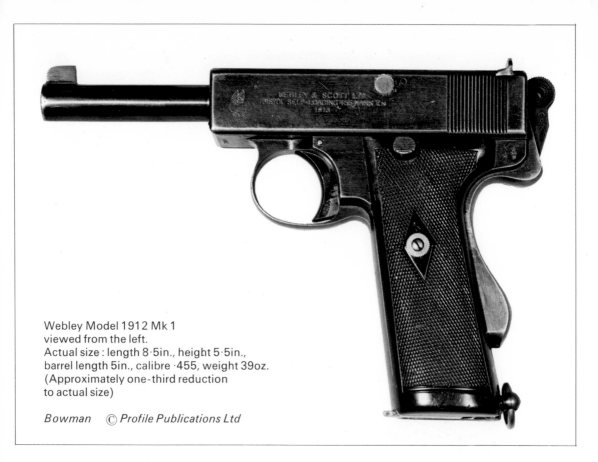

Webley Model 1912 Mk 1
viewed from the left.
Actual size : length 8·5in., height 5·5in.,
barrel length 5in., calibre ·455, weight 39oz.
(Approximately one-third reduction
to actual size)

Bowman © *Profile Publications Ltd*

Webley Model 1912 Mk 1
viewed from the right.
Actual size : length 8·5in., height 5·5in.,
barrel length 5in., calibre ·455, weight 39oz
(Approximately one-third reduction
to actual size)

Bowman © *Profile Publications Ltd*

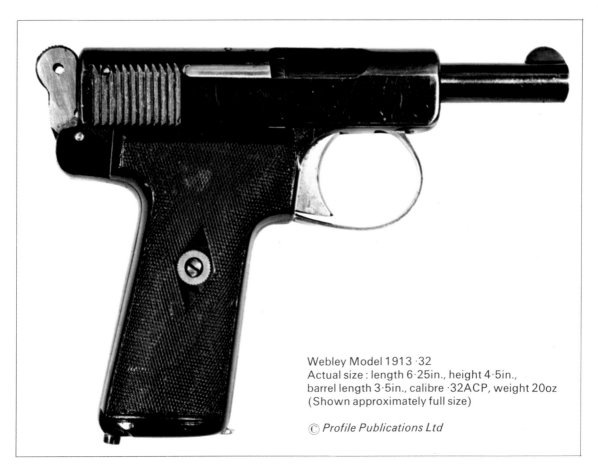

Webley Model 1913 ·32
Actual size : length 6·25in., height 4·5in.,
barrel length 3·5in., calibre ·32ACP, weight 20oz
(Shown approximately full size)

© *Profile Publications Ltd*

Webley ·22 long barrel with shoulder stock
Actual size : length 11 in., height 4·5in.,
barrel length 9in., calibre ·22L.R., weight 23¾oz
(Shown here approximately half size)

Bowman © *Profile Publications Ltd*

Beretta Model 318 Gold Plated frame

Pattern Room, Enfield   © *Profile Publications Ltd*

The Authors Model 1934 Beretta

© *Profile Publications Ltd*

Beretta 1934 with magazine out and slide forward

© *Profile Publications Ltd*

Beretta 1934 with slide to rear   © *Profile Publications Ltd*

An Engraver at work in the Astra factory. On the bench, a Pistol fully engraved, Shotgun parts, and Pistol parts to be engraved

Courtesy of Astra
© Profile Publications Limited

Part of the Astra Machine shop where a Broach is at work. Racks of Shotgun barrels and Revolver frames can be seen

Courtesy of Astra
© Profile Publications Limited

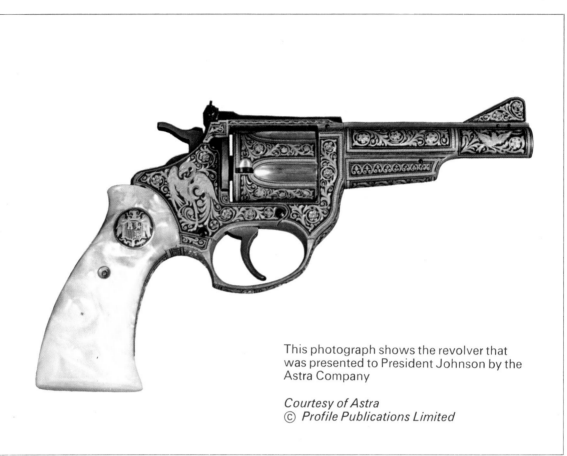

This photograph shows the revolver that was presented to President Johnson by the Astra Company

Courtesy of Astra
© *Profile Publications Limited*

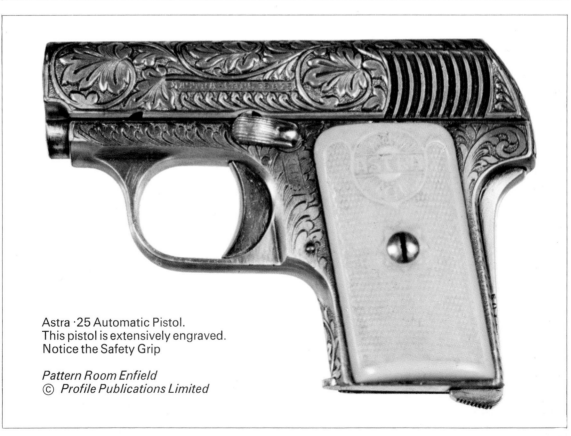

Astra ·25 Automatic Pistol.
This pistol is extensively engraved.
Notice the Safety Grip

Pattern Room Enfield
© *Profile Publications Limited*

Left side of Beretta Model 1919. Notice the grip safety

Right side of Model 1919. Notice the simple sighting arrangement

Model 1915/19 Calibre 7·65mm

The Model 1915/19 is, as its designation indicates, a modification of the 7·65mm (·32ACP) Model 1915. The basic weapon remains identical with the addition of a modified magazine with a grip extension, a simpler and easier to operate safety catch and a larger ejection port. The barrel attachment was changed from a vertical slot in the model 1915 to the standard horizontal one. This pistol, which was to continue as the only 7·65mm Beretta until 1931, was issued to the Army, the Navy (Regia Marina) and the Air Force (Regia Aeronautica).

Model 1919 6·35mm

With the success of the Browning small calibre automatic pistols (see Profile No. 2) Beretta decided that there was a market for a 6·35mm pistol. The pistol follows the basic design of the Model 15/19 but incorporates a grip safety. The weapon is smaller in overall dimensions than the Model 15/19 but otherwise apart from the grip safety is externally the same.

Model 1923 9mm Glisenti

This pistol was only produced in relatively small quantities and as a result is rare. It is chambered for

the 9mm Glisenti and the same warnings apply as for the Model 1915. Unlike the previous models the 1923 has an external hammer. Few, if any, were sold in the commercial market and most went to the Army with the Mark RE. The magazine contains eight rounds and has a catch at the rear of the grip. A few weapons were fitted with a holster shoulder stock.

Model 318 6·35mm

This pistol is based on the Model 1919 and apart from an improved grip angle and shape is little different. The stocks are made of bakelite as opposed to wooden ones on the Model 1919.

Model 1931 7·65mm

This pistol although very similar in shape to the Model 1915/19 has an external hammer. As the weapon was made almost exclusively for the Italian Navy, on most weapons the grips carry the monogram RM (Regia Marina). However, a few were sold on the commercial market. The development of the 1931 bridges the gap between the Model 1923 and the ultimate 1934. On the Model 1931 the safety which only locks the trigger, is not to be relied on as the hammer could be jarred from the sear and the weapon fired. It is

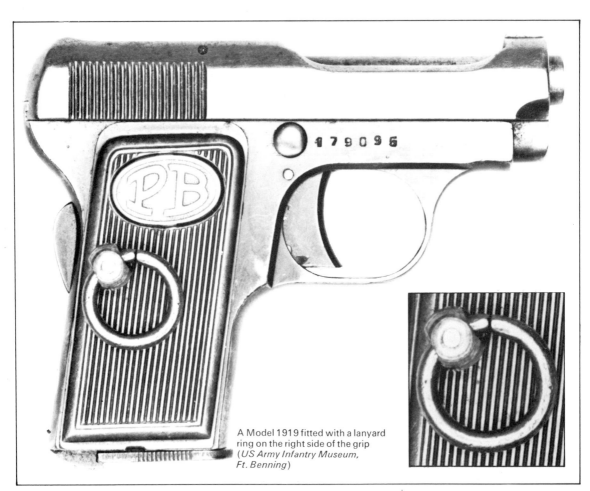

A Model 1919 fitted with a lanyard ring on the right side of the grip (*US Army Infantry Museum, Ft. Benning*)

Model 1923 Beretta chambered for 9mm short. Notice the RE emblem at the top rear of the frame (*Pattern Room, Enfield*)

Right side of Model 1923 showing the longer grip
which distinguishes this weapon from its predecessors
(*Pattern Room, Enfield*)

A Model 1931 Beretta chambered for
7·65mm cartridge showing clearly the
RM monogram on the butt
(*Pattern Room, Enfield*)

Right side of the Model 1931 Beretta
showing the RM monogram and the grip
extension   (*Pattern Room, Enfield*)

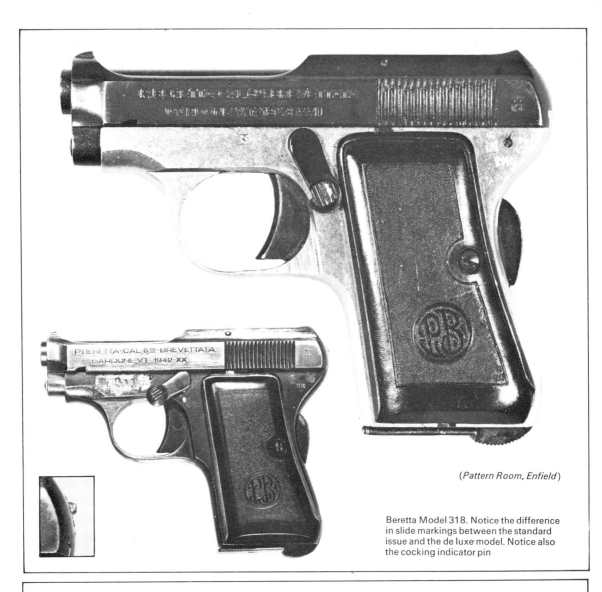

(Pattern Room, Enfield)

Beretta Model 318. Notice the difference in slide markings between the standard issue and the de luxe model. Notice also the cocking indicator pin

The right side of the Model 318. Notice the grip safety and the PB emblem

The left side of the Beretta Model 1934.
This weapon was carried by many of the
Italian forces throughout World War II.
Notice the difference between the
slide milling on the two weapons and
also the RE and Eagle monograms on
the rear frame

(*Pattern Room, Enfield*)

therefore recommended that with a chambered
round care is taken.

Model 1934 9mm Court (·380ACP)

This pistol which is a development of the Model
1931 is the best known of the Beretta production.
It served as the sidearm of the Italian Army
throughout World War II and was not replaced until
the adoption of the Model 951 in 9mm parabellum.
The 1934 however is still in production today under
the trade name COUGAR. It is a well made reliable
pistol which suffers the only disadvantage of being
chambered for a cartridge which can barely be called

an effective military one.

As with all Beretta pistols the 1934 has a straight
blowback operation with recoil spring situated under
the barrel. The barrel is removable and is held in
place by the safety and slots in the frame making the
pistol easy to strip for cleaning. The sights are fixed,
the front one being part of the slide and the rear one
dovetailed into it. A seven-round magazine with a
grip extension is used with the release at the rear of
the butt. The slide markings vary with the date of
manufacture and incorporate Roman numerals.
These Roman numerals indicate the date of
production on the Fascist calendar which starts at

Left side of the Model 1934 Beretta

An experimental model 1934
Beretta fitted with slide mounted
safety catch
(*Pattern Room, Enfield*)

The lightweight Model 1934 Beretta
(*Pattern Room, Enfield*)

the year One in 1922.

One interesting Model 1934 examined by the author would seem to have been an attempt to cut down the weight as the weapon is lighter than the standard one and has a thinner slide. Markings to be found on the 1934 include RE (Regia Esercito) Royal Army : PS (Publica Sicurezza) Police Use. The cartridge is known as 9mm Model 34 in Italy and 9mm short or ·380 ACP elsewhere. This weapon can also be known as the Model 934. Many Beretta weapons are known by either the Model date in full or the last three figures (1934=934).

Model 1935 7·65mm

This pistol is the same as the 1934 but chambered for the 7·65mm ·32 ACP round. It is hard to understand the change to a round which is even less a military cartridge than the ·380 ACP as it is the lowest powered cartridge to exhibit any stopping power. With this in mind, the adoption of the weapon by the Italian Air Force and marked AM or RA (Aeronautica Militare or Regia Aeronautica) the Italian Navy and marked RM (Regia Marina) is extraordinary. The weapon was also sold commercially as the Model 935. This Model was replaced by the Model 70 in 1958.

Model 418 6·35mm

This pistol is the successor to the 318 on which production was stopped in 1946. The 418 which is also called the Puma is modernised by streamlining the shape, a modified grip safety and the manual safety placed on the left side of the receiver. An indicator pin is fitted on the slide which shows when the weapon is cocked, thus eliminating one of the drawbacks of a hammerless or concealed hammer weapon. This weapon was superseded when production stopped in 1951 by the Model 950.

Model 948 ·22LR

This weapon, which is dimensionally identical to the Model 1934 is chambered for the ·22 Long Rifle. The only modifications are in the firing pin and the magazine. It is available with two alternative barrel lengths. Production was stopped in 1958. The Model 949 ·22LR is a pure target pistol and therefore outside the scope of this Profile.

Model 950 6·35mm

This pistol which was brought on the market in 1950 has one peculiarity which sets it aside from all other Beretta pistols. This pistol has the odd feature of being either a single-shot breech loader or a

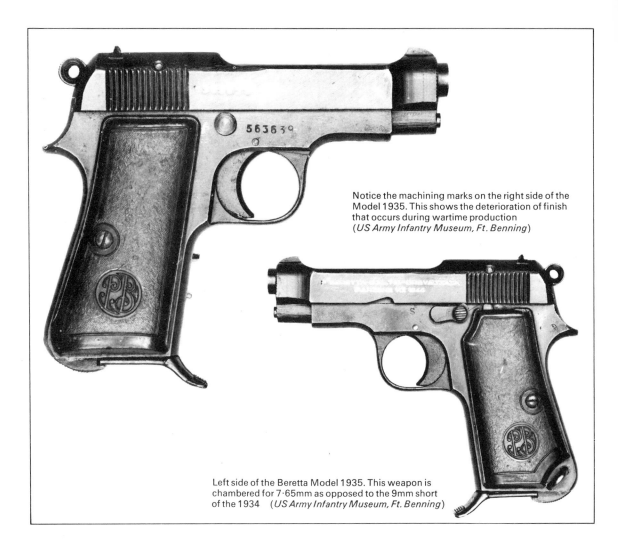

Notice the machining marks on the right side of the Model 1935. This shows the deterioration of finish that occurs during wartime production (*US Army Infantry Museum, Ft. Benning*)

Left side of the Beretta Model 1935. This weapon is chambered for 7·65mm as opposed to the 9mm short of the 1934 (*US Army Infantry Museum, Ft. Benning*)

magazine-fed automatic. The single shot ability is achieved by making the barrel hinge upward from the front enabling a round to be chambered. With the barrel in the downward position the weapon functions as a normal pistol. The weapon has an external hammer and the receiver is made of light alloy although the slide is high-grade steel. There is no separate ejector and the pistol utilises residue gas pressure to blow out the empty case. No safety catch is fitted although there is a half-cock notch for the hammer. The pistol was modified after the initial announcement and named the 950B. In the USA the weapon is sold under the name of MINX. The 950 is available chambered for the ·22 short with either a 60mm barrel or a 95mm barrel (950B special). Also marketed is a range of 950 models with engraving, gold, silver or chrome finishes.

Model 70 Series

The Model 70 series are designed to replace the Model 1935 and Model 948 with a more streamlined and modern weapon. The Model 70 which replaced the 935 in 1958 can be obtained with either a steel or light alloy receiver, chambered for the 7·65mm (·32 ACP). The Model 70 as with all 70 series pistols

is blowback operated. The barrel mounting is composed of a larger slide area. The safety catch is at the rear of the slide, convenient for the thumb and blocks both hammer and sear when the weapon is cocked. A slide lock is fitted which is actuated by the magazine follower and holds the slide open on the last shot. This combined with a magazine release button which is easily operated makes the pistol particularly easy to reload. The Model 70 is sold under the name of PUMA in the USA. The other weapons in the 70 Series are identical except in calibre and are as follows:

71—This is the same as the Model 70 but chambered for the ·22LR with a 90mm barrel

72—The same as the Model 71 but supplied with two barrels— one for defence (90mm) and one for target practice of 150mm. (The ·22LR hardly qualifies as a defence cartridge). This is called the JAGUAR in the USA.

73-74-75—Pure target pistols of the cheaper variety.

Model 20 ·25 ACP

This pistol is an improvement on the Model 950B. It features a double-action trigger for the first time on a Beretta. It has a thumb safety and a button magazine release.

The ·22 Long Rifle Model 948 Beretta. Notice the change in the grip design   (*Pattern Room, Enfield*)

Beretta Model 950 and Model 950 special. These weapons are identical except for the barrel length. Notice the slide markings on the longer barrelled 950 giving its American name 'Minx' (*Pattern Room, Enfield*)

Right side of Model 950. Notice the 'Made in Italy' stamped on the side and the different grip emblem (*Pattern Room, Enfield*)

Model 90

This weapon departs even more from the established shape of the 1934 than the Model 70 and clearly follows that of the Walther PP/PPK range.
This pistol also featured the Walther system of using the barrel as a recoil spring guide. The trigger is double action for the first shot and the safety is on the left side of the frame.

Model 1951 9mm parabellum

This is the only pistol in the Beretta range past or present to feature a locked breech. The system employed is similar to that employed in the Walther P38. It is similar in outline to the Model 1934 but longer overall. The safety is a push-through button positioned under the rear of the slide.

The weapon is made in four basic variants ; the M1951 as the standard weapon for the Italian Army and Navy ; the BRIGADIER for commercial sale, the Egyptian Army Model with their coat of arms and the Egyptian target model with target sights and wood grips. It can be obtained with a steel receiver only. The line of Beretta pistols have always had the quality which comes from a firm of long family traditions of good workmanship. The factory has survived every manner of dispute, war and insurrection and can be expected to continue manufacturing first-class weapons of high finish for a long time to come.

Model	Calibre	Length	Barrel Length	Magazine Capacity	Weight
1915	7·65mm	149mm	85mm	7	610gr
1915	9mm	169mm	95mm	8	975gr
1915/19	7·65mm			8	
1919	6·35mm	114mm	60mm	8	390gr
1923	9mm			8	
318	6·35mm	115mm	60mm	8	425gr
1934	9mm court	150mm	88mm	7	750gr
1935	7·65mm	148mm	85mm	8	730gr
418	6·35mm	116mm	60mm	8	335gr
950	6·35mm	118mm	60mm	8	320gr
950 Special	6·35mm	154mm	95mm	8	340gr
70	7·65mm	165mm	90mm	8	575gr
951	9mm	204mm	114mm	8-10	820gr
90	·32 ACP	6·7"	3·6"	8	19·4oz

The Beretta Model 951. Notice the difference in finish between the two versions and the difference in the magazine release catch *(Pattern Room, Enfield)*

Left and right sides of the Model 70 Beretta. Notice the
continuing basic shape. This weapon is chambered for the
7·65mm (·32ACP) round   (*Beretta*)

950 Model Beretta shown with the superlative
factory engraving   (*Beretta*)

The Model 20 calibre 6·35mm (·25ACP) Beretta pistol.
Although retaining the basic shape this pistol features a
double action trigger   (*Beretta*)

The Model 90 double action 7·65mm Beretta pistol. Notice the
complete departure from the well established shape
(*Beretta*)

Right side of the 9mm parabellum Beretta Model 951. This is a military production weapon (*Pattern Room, Enfield*)

A characteristic of many Beretta pistols is the magazine mounted grip extension (*From a model 1934*)

A presentation ·25 Astra Pistol. Notice the extremely intricate damascene work

(Weller & Dufty)

Astra Pistols and Revolvers
by A. J. R. Cormack

A number of firms, Astra being one of them, have always belied the myth that all Spanish firearms are of poor quality. The weapons produced from the company's founding at the turn of the century have always been of the highest quality.

Pedro Unceta y Juan Esperenza as the Astra Company was first known was founded in Eibar in Spain in 1908. Their first production was of an automatic pistol called the Victoria. Pedro Unceta was behind the overall administration of the company and Juan Esperenza handled the production side.

In 1913 the company changed its name to Esperenza y Unceta and owing to lack of production space the factory was moved to Guernica. At the same time Pedro Unceta, Don Pedro's son joined the firm to continue the family name.

At Guernica the Victoria pistol was produced in a number of different variants.

From 1904 Count Giro had been experimenting with a series of automatic pistols and in 1914 the Spanish Army adopted the Campogiro Model 1913 and requested that Esperenza y Unceta produce them. In 1914 the firm also adopted the name Astra, a name that has remained as the Registered Mark of the company. Under the registered name of Astra many thousands of pistols were exported to France and Italy. In 1920 the first of the small Browning type pistols was put into production and in 1921 an Astra pistol, the Model 400, became the official sidearm of the Spanish Army. This pistol was the first to have the typical Astra 'water pistol' type of outline. Both this and the earlier pistol were to continue in production in modified forms until late into the 1960s. The company's name was once again changed when in

143

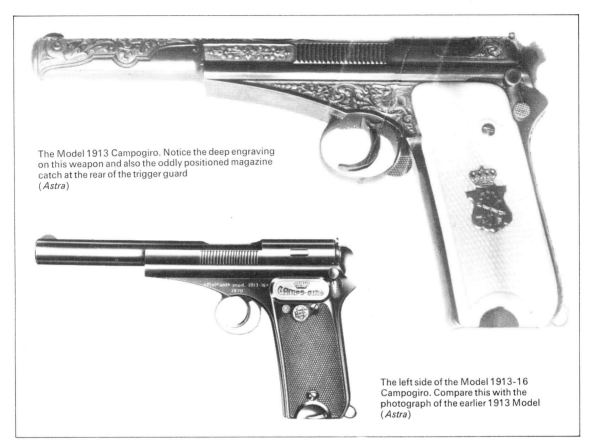

The Model 1913 Campogiro. Notice the deep engraving on this weapon and also the oddly positioned magazine catch at the rear of the trigger guard (*Astra*)

The left side of the Model 1913-16 Campogiro. Compare this with the photograph of the earlier 1913 Model (*Astra*)

1926 it adopted Unceta y Compania. After a brief period of time spent developing submachine guns for the Spanish Army under the name of Astra-Union, they in 1928 produced the first of the Mauser-shaped machine pistols. With the outbreak of war a number of different weapons were developed and with the German capacity for production being insufficient, Astra supplied first the Model 400 and later the 9mm parabellum development Model 600 to the German Army. After the war the firm branched out from the pure weapons factory to one producing textile accessories and pneumatic hammers. In 1953 the company once again changed its name, this time to Astra Unceta y Cia. From this time on modifications to the basic designs continued to flow from the Factory with the production in 1958 of the first of the revolvers and in 1969 the first double-action pistol.

Campogiro

Count Giro developed a number of different basic variants of a pistol, starting with a locked breech weapon, the Model 1904. This was the first patented weapon and was manufactured in small numbers with many variations. The locking system is a wedge type with a wedge that locks at the rear of the barrel. The locking is controlled by a cam. The pistol has a box magazine with 8 rounds contained in the butt. Between 1904 and 1910 development continued and a further weapon, the Model 1910 was manufactured. Both the Model 1904 and Model 1910 were manufactured at the Oviedo Arsenal, 1000 Model 1910s being produced. Count Giro's

last patent was for the Campogiro Model 1913 which unlike its predecessors was of a delayed blowback design. This delay is produced by the replacement of the locking wedge piece with a spring loaded buffer plate. The weapon is nearly identical with the earlier types apart from this and the addition of a safety catch on the frame. The complete range of Campogiro pistols have the recoil spring round the barrel, a feature that many of the Astra pistols were to use. Both this pistol and a development, the Model 1913/16 were manufactured in some quantity by Esperenza y Unceta. Production ceased in 1921. A major difference between the Model 1913 and the Model 1913/16 is that the magazine catch on the 1913 is fitted under the frame at the rear of the trigger guard. All the Campogiro pistols were chambered for the 9mm Largo round. The 9mm Largo round is also known as the Bergman Bayard. It is a rimless straight sided case of similar power (in a modern loading) to the ·38 ACP (old load 1000 fps, modern 1100 fps). The basic dimensions of the models are as follows:

Barrel length	1910	6·7 inches
	1913	6·7 inches
Total length	1910	10·7 inches
	1913	9·7 inches
	1913/16	8·9 inches
Weight	1913	2·1lbs
	1913/16	2·2lbs
Height	1913	130mm
	1913/16	135mm
Mag capacity	1913	8 rounds
	1913/16	8 rounds

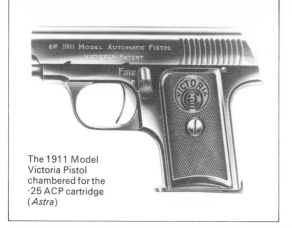

The 1911 Model Victoria Pistol chambered for the ·25 ACP cartridge (*Astra*)

This model 1911 ·32 ACP has a concealed hammer. This view shows the safety catch in the safety position (*Pattern Room, Enfield*)

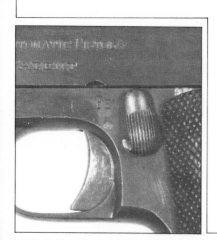

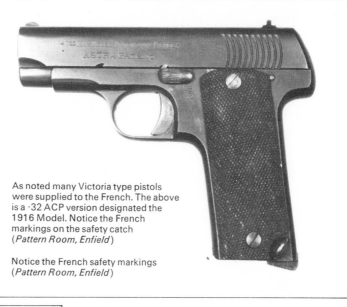

As noted many Victoria type pistols were supplied to the French. The above is a ·32 ACP version designated the 1916 Model. Notice the French markings on the safety catch (*Pattern Room, Enfield*)

Notice the French safety markings (*Pattern Room, Enfield*)

The ·32 ACP Model 1911 Victoria with an external hammer. Notice the English safety catch markings (*Astra*)

The Victoria (**Model 1911**)

Production of the Victoria started in 1908. This is a ·25 ACP or ·32 ACP pistol having no noteworthy features. It is a straight blowback weapon similar to the small Brownings. It was produced in a number of variations, one of which was supplied to the Italian armed forces and in 1914 a further variation was supplied to the French armed forces. Production was suspended just after the end of World War I. The dimensions are:

	·25 ACP	·32 ACP
Overall length	4·29 inches	5·79 inches
Barrel length	2·17 inches	3·23 inches
Weight	11·53 ozs	21·3 ozs
Magazine capacity	7 rounds	6 rounds

A large number of pistols of the Victoria type were also manufactured under a variety of names. The names encountered are as follows:

T.E.	Muxi	Fortuna
Manufacture Lugeuse d'Armes	Salso	Caminal
The Automatic Leston	Scot	Boix

The production totalled some 35,500.

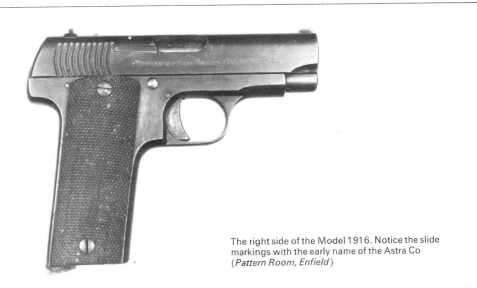

The right side of the Model 1916. Notice the slide markings with the early name of the Astra Co (*Pattern Room, Enfield*)

The left side of the ·25 ACP Model 200 Astra. Notice the loaded indicator pin on the rear of the slide (*Astra*)

This pistol is the Firecat which is identical to the Model 200. Production was stopped in 1967 (*Astra*)

A Model 200 or Firecat with the full engraving—silver plated (*Astra*)

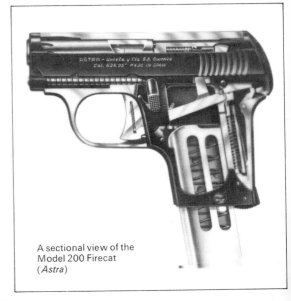

A sectional view of the Model 200 Firecat (*Astra*)

Astra Browning Types

This group of weapons all bear a resemblance to the typical small Browning blowback pistol and the Victoria and in most features are identical. A Browning type of pistol was also manufactured under the name 'Union'.

Union

All three of the Union models follow the well-tried Browning type. Models 1 and 2 are in ·25 ACP and Model 3 in ·32 ACP. The dimensions of the weapons are as follows:

	Vestpocket Model 1	Pocket Model 2	Pocket Model 3
Length	11·5cm	11·5cm	14·5cm
Height	7·5cm	10·0cm	9·5cm
Weight	385g	445g	700g
Magazine capacity	6 rounds	9 rounds	7 rounds

Production quantities of this weapon are unfortunately unknown. It is also possible that a number of Smith & Wesson type revolvers were manufactured under the Union name.

Model 100

The Model 100 is chambered for the 7·65mm ·32 ACP cartridge and as noted follows the classic Browning lines. It has an overall length of 6 inches with a barrel length of 3·34 inches. It has a nine round magazine which is contained in the butt. The total weight is 1lb 13ozs.

Model 200 and Firecat

The Model 200 was designed in 1920 and continued in production under the Firecat name until 1966. The 200 and the Firecat use the ·25 ACP cartridge. It is of simple blowback design having a concealed hammer. A thumb safety is located on the left hand side and this operates directly on the trigger, preventing any movement. A magazine safety is also fitted which stops the firing of the weapon until a magazine is in place. In a similar fashion to some of the Browning designs a grip safety is also fitted. In addition to the above safety features an indicator pin protrudes from the rear of the slide when the pistol is loaded and the hammer cocked for firing, thus at any time, night or day, the condition of the weapon can be checked by not only sight but also touch. The overall length of the weapon is $4\frac{1}{3}$ inches, the height 3 inches and the length of the barrel $2\frac{1}{5}$ inches. The magazine capacity is six rounds and the weapon weighs with the magazine $11\frac{4}{5}$ ounces. A number of variants designated 200/1/2/3 were available as was the case with the Firecat. The designation merely means the type of finish and degree of decoration.

Model 1000

A further variant known as the Model 1000 has been produced having a 12 round magazine and being chambered for the ·32 ACP round.
The pistols in standard form are 200mm long, barrel length 130mm, height 140mm, and weight 1050g.

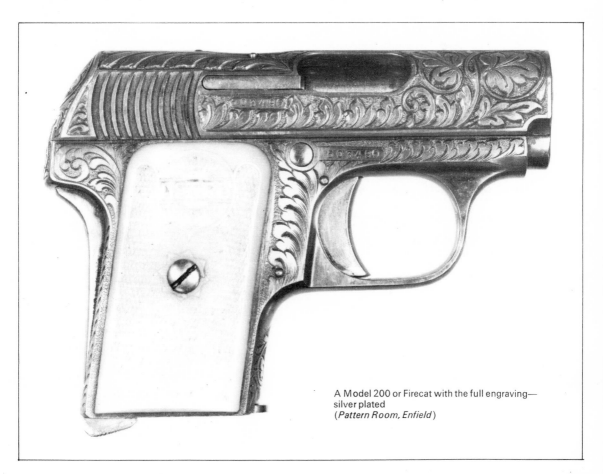

A Model 200 or Firecat with the full engraving—silver plated
(*Pattern Room, Enfield*)

The Model 1000 Special varies only in that the overall length is 170mm and the barrel 106mm. Astra continued their production of Browning types with a series called the Cub and the Camper. The most interesting of the series is however the pistol called the Colt Junior.

Colt Junior

The Colt company in the 1950s felt the financial loss from the lack of a small defence pistol to combat the large volume of imports. Colt deciding that it was not economic in production space or development costs to develop a pistol of their own, contacted Astra to supply a ready-developed pistol. The pistol was available in two calibres, ·22 short and ·25 ACP. A conversion kit that is very rare was available to convert the ·25 ACP to ·22 short. There were a total of 67,000 weapons imported between 1957 and 1968. The new strict American gun laws finally stopped the importation by Colt. The frame of the pistol is marked on the right side 'Made in Spain for Colt'. Dimensions of the weapon are as follows:

Length	4¾ inches
Barrel length	2¼ inches
Both magazines take 7 rounds	

Astra Cub and Camper (Model 2000)

This weapon is the Spanish market version of the Colt Junior. The pistol has an external hammer and both a magazine safety and a hammer safety. The choice of calibre for defensive use is poor as both cartridges may be lethal under ideal conditions but neither can be considered effective. The Camper is a long barrelled version of the Cub—101mm as opposed to 57mm. Production of the Camper stopped in 1966.

The Colt Junior Model. This pistol is identical to the Astra Model Cub (*Astra*)

The ·25 ACP Model Cub in its standard form (*Astra*)

The left side of the Model 2000. This pistol is chambered for the ·22 Short (*Pattern Room, Enfield*)

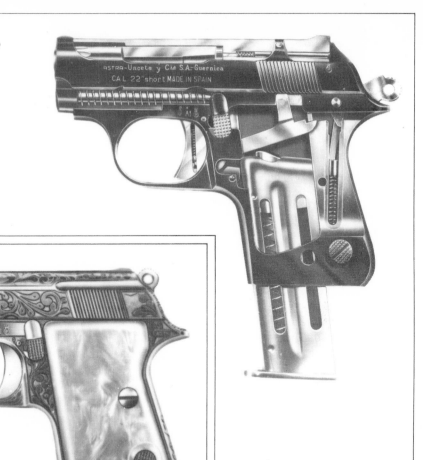

A sectioned model 2000 Cub
chambered for ·22 Short
(*Astra*)

The Model 2000 Cub, engraved and
silver-plated
(*Astra*)

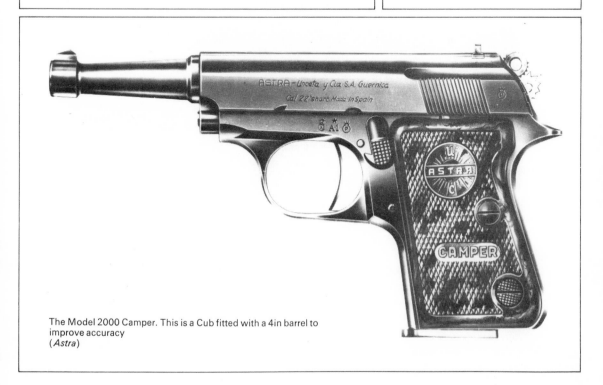

The Model 2000 Camper. This is a Cub fitted with a 4in barrel to
improve accuracy
(*Astra*)

Model 7000

This pistol which entered production in 1972 is of the small Browning type and is chambered for the ·22 Long Rifle cartridge. The dimensions are as follows:

Total length	125mm
Barrel length	59·4mm
Height	88mm
Weight	390g
Magazine capacity	7 rounds

Between 1954 and 1970 a staggering 295,973 pistols of all models were produced.

Astra Tubular Slide Type
Model 300 and 3000

This pistol which was first produced in 1923 is an adaptation of the Model 400. The weapon has the distinctive 'water pistol' shape of all the Campogiro developed Astra pistols which have the recoil spring round the barrel. All this type of Astra are blowback or retarded blowback in operation. The 300 is chambered for either the ·32 or ·380 cartridges. The weapon was adopted as the standard sidearm of the high ranking officers of the Spanish Navy (La Marina Espanola) with a military designation of 1928A, and the Spanish prison service (Cuerpo de Prisiones). During the war years the German army, who had a high respect for Spanish weapons, produced by Astra and Star, ordered 85,390 Model 300 pistols. Between 1941

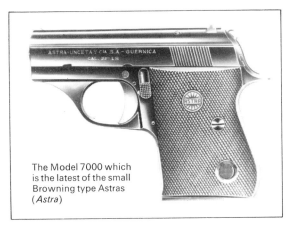

The Model 7000 which is the latest of the small Browning type Astras (*Astra*)

and 1944, 22,390 ·380 ACP pistols and 63,000 ·380 ACP pistols were delivered. Manufacture of the model 300 was stopped in 1947 after a total of 171,300 had been produced. The basic dimensions of the weapon are:

Overall length	165mm
Barrel length	90mm
Height	100mm
Weight	560g
Magazine capacity	·32 ACP—7 rounds ·380 ACP—6 rounds

Between 1948 and 1956 production of the Model 300 was resumed under the designation Model 3000. A total of 26,700 were produced in

The right side of the Model 300 Astra. Notice the grip safety (*Astra*)

A silver plated and fully engraved Model 3000 Astra. Notice the cartridge loaded pin at the rear of the slide (*Astra*)

this slightly modified form. A chamber loaded indicator was fitted. When the chamber is loaded a pin projects from the rear of the slide. The dimensions are as follows:

Model 3000	
Overall length	160mm
Length of barrel	101·5mm
Height	103mm
Weight	620g
Magazine capacity	·32 ACP—7 rounds
	·380 ACP—6 rounds

Model 400 (Modelo 1921)

This pistol was the first of the tubular slide type and entered production in 1921. The basic design was based on the Campogiro and retained the basic features of the barrel with the recoil spring fitted round its outside. However, the barrel had a different mounting system and the weapon could be dismantled without any tools.

Early production weapons had a buffer system similar to that of the Campogiro. This was soon dropped however and the weapon functioned as a straight blowback which, because of the highpowered cartridges utilised, necessitates extremely heavy recoil and hammer springs. The weapon has a magazine safety, and a grip safety as well as the normal slide safety. The cartridge which the weapon was specifically designed for was the same as that of the Campogiro, the 9mm Largo (9mm Bergman Bayard). However, Astra claim that various cartridges such as 9mm parabellum, ·38 ACP, 9mm Steyre and even 9mm short can be fired in the weapon. The author has seen tests however which while proving that the cartridges all *may* be fired, in most cases because of the lack of head spacing it is certainly not in any manner as efficient as with the correct cartridge and not to be recommended.

In August 1921 the Spanish Army organised a competitive trial to determine which pistol would succeed the Campogiro. Owing to its exceptional durability during this trial the Astra Model 400 was accepted as the regulation sidearm of the Spanish Army, under the designation Pistola de 9mm Model 1921. This was on 6 October 1921. During the years that followed it was also accepted by most state organisations: Guardia Civil (Civil Guard), Carabineros (Police) and Marina (Marines). An export programme was a great success as Germany, Colombia, Chile, Ecuador, Salvador, and others purchased the weapon.

During 1941, 6000 Model 400 Astras were sold to the German army. Further sales were hoped for but the chambering being for other than the standard 9mm parabellum round stopped them. Production stopped in 1945 when a total of 106,175 pistols had been produced. The dimensions of the weapon are:

Length	8·7 inches
Barrel length	5·9 inches
Weight with magazine	2lbs
Magazine capacity	8 rounds

The Model 400 Astra Tubular Slide Type chambered for the 9mm Largo round
(*Pattern Room, Enfield*)

The right side of the Model 21 or 400. Notice the difference between this weapon's grips and that of the previous illustration
(*Pattern Room, Enfield*)

Falcon (Model 4000)

In 1956 a new pistol based on the Model 400 was announced. This was named the Model 4000 Series and given a trade name 'Falcon'. The Falcon is available in three calibres—7·65 ; ·32 ACP and 9mm short—·380 ACP for defence use and in ·22 Long rifle for practice. The weapon has no grip safety, however the magazine safety is retained. Because of the lighter calibres the weapon is reduced in size having a total barrel length of $3\frac{2}{3}$ inches, length 6·5 inches, height $4\frac{1}{3}$ inches and it weighs 24ozs. In ·32 ACP the magazine holds 8 rounds, ·380 7 rounds, 22LR 10 rounds. An experimental version, the 4000 with a square slide and frame was produced in the 1950s but not adopted for production.

Model 400 Copies

The Spanish Civil War had a similar effect on weapon design to that of the American Civil War where one side not being in possession of a factory having an indigenous weapon copied one of the other side's types and produced it. Two copies of the Astra Model 400 were manufactured in the Republican Zone, one in Valencia under the initials RE (Republica Espanol) and the other in Catalonia with the mark F Ascaso who was a famous anarchist fighter. It is not known what production quantities were achieved, however it is thought that some 12,000 pistols were surrendered to the German Army in 1941.

Model 500

The Model 500 is similar to the Model 400 but is chambered for the 9mm Browning long cartridge. The overall length is reduced to 7·1 inches. (This model designation is doubtful, as Astra have no records of the production.)

Model 600 (600/43)

In 1943 the German Government, happy with the other Astra pistols purchased and short of home production, asked Astra to produce a modified Model 400 for the 9mm parabellum cartridge. Fifty prototypes were assembled with smaller frames and grip safeties. The delivery of the pistols was easy as the Germans occupied France up to the Spanish border. In 1944, 10,450 pistols with the designation Pistol Astra 600/43 were delivered. However, the follow-up order for 28,000 were never delivered as the Germans had retreated. These pistols had been manufactured and so even after the war when production had ceased (59,546 being made) the pistols remained in Spain. The German Federal Republic, needing a pistol for their police force, and having no production facilities after the war, purchased many of these remaining weapons. The dimensions of the Model 600 are as follows :

| Total length | 205mm | Weight | 990g |
| Barrel length | 134mm | Magazine capacity | 8 cartridges |

Model 700 and 700 Special

This pistol is one of the few produced by Astra to achieve only small production quantities as only 4000 were produced in 1926. It has the typical water-pistol features and the dimensions are as follows :

	Model 700	Model 700 Special
Calibre	·32 ACP	·32 ACP
Barrel length	150mm	95mm
Total length	215mm	160mm
Height	125mm	125mm
Weight	725g	725g
Magazine capacity	8 rounds	9 or 12 rounds

An official German instructional poster of the Astra Model 400

(*Astra*)

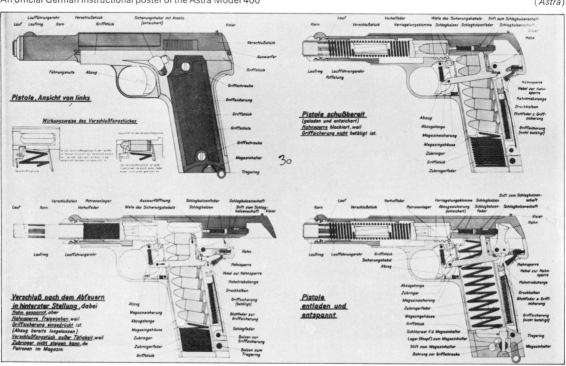

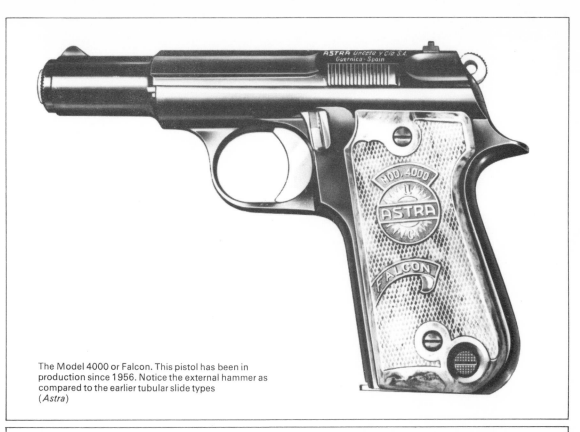

The Model 4000 or Falcon. This pistol has been in production since 1956. Notice the external hammer as compared to the earlier tubular slide types (*Astra*)

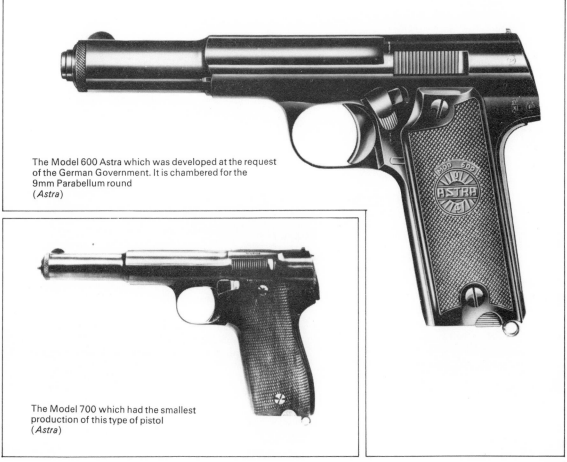

The Model 600 Astra which was developed at the request of the German Government. It is chambered for the 9mm Parabellum round (*Astra*)

The Model 700 which had the smallest production of this type of pistol (*Astra*)

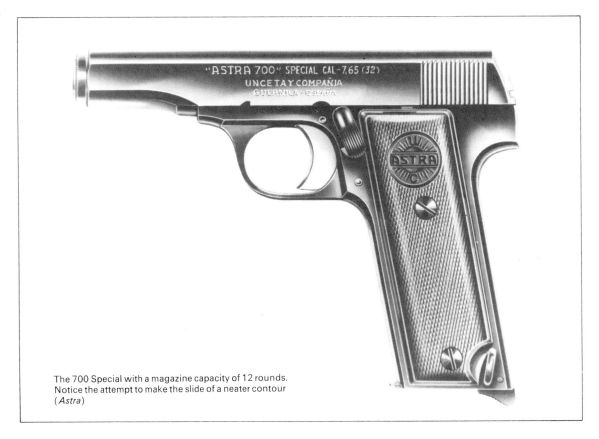

The 700 Special with a magazine capacity of 12 rounds.
Notice the attempt to make the slide of a neater contour
(*Astra*)

Model 800 or Condor

In 1958 Astra announced a new design based on
the tubular slide type. This was the Model 800 or
Condor. The main differences from the earlier type
are the use of an external hammer and a loaded
indicator pin. A magazine safety is also fitted.
This pistol is chambered for the 9mm Parabellum
round and as it is a simple blowback design an
extremely strong recoil spring is fitted. Production
ceased in 1966 after 11,432 pistols had been
produced. The dimensions are as follows:

Length	207mm
Barrel length	134mm
Height	130mm
Weight	1000g
Magazine capacity	8 rounds

Astra Mauser-Type Pistols

A number of Spanish copies of the German Mauser
1896 'Broomhandle' were manufactured. One of the
best is the Astra 900 series. The external design of the
pistol is very similar to the Mauser but the internal
mechanism differs. The locking piece is pinned to
the barrel extension unlike that of the Mauser. The
weapon has a detachable side plate through which
the weapon is stripped. The early weapons were clip
loaded as with the Mauser, but like the Mauser
rapid-fire version the later pistols could be loaded by
a detachable magazine as well as the clip. The
magazine is in front of the grip in a similar fashion to
that of the Mauser. The weapon was supplied with a
hollowed-out shoulder stock holster. All versions
are produced to a high standard. The Series
consists of the following:

Model 900—this pistol is semi-automatic fire only
and was developed from a series of patents taken
out in 1928. Production of this pistol was carried out
between 1928 and 1937 during which time
34,325 were produced. Some 30,000 of these were
exported to China with the legend 'Astra China
Company' stamped on the pistol. The Model 900
was also adopted by the Policia de Seguridad and
the Guardia Civil. It is chambered for the Mauser 7·63
pistol cartridge and has a 10-shot capacity.
Model 1901—this weapon is selective fire (the
selector is on the right side of the frame) and has a
10-shot magazine for a 7·63 Mauser cartridge.
Model 1902—this is merely a 20-shot version of the
Model 901. The Model 903 introduces the
detachable magazine, however, the weapon can
still be loaded from clips. A version, the 903E,
enabled only semi-automatic fire. Both versions
have either a 10 or 20 shot magazine and can be
chambered for either 7·63 Mauser or 9mm Largo.
Model F—this version was chambered for the 9mm
Largo and had an additional retarder fitted. It has a
detachable magazine of either 10 or 20 shots.
Approximately 2000 of the Model F were supplied to
the Guardia Civil. All the 900 and F Series pistols
were produced between the years 1928 and 1937.
The dimensions of the Astra 900 Series are:

	Model 900	Model 903	Model F
Length	290mm	308mm	13 inches
Barrel length	140mm	160mm	7·19 inches
Length with stock	640mm	685mm	27·25 inches
Height	150mm	150mm	—
Weight	1260g	1275g	3lbs 6ozs
Weight with stock	1700g		

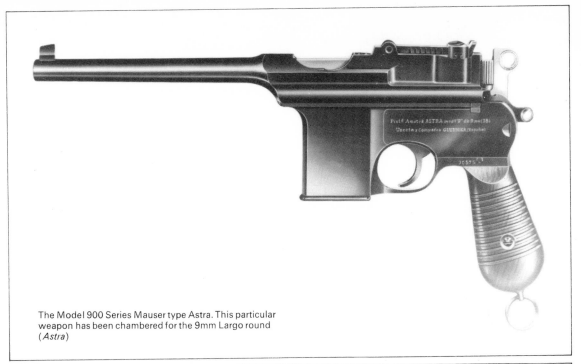

The Model 900 Series Mauser type Astra. This particular
weapon has been chambered for the 9mm Largo round
(*Astra*)

A Model 900 Astra fitted with
shoulder stock holster
(*Astra*)

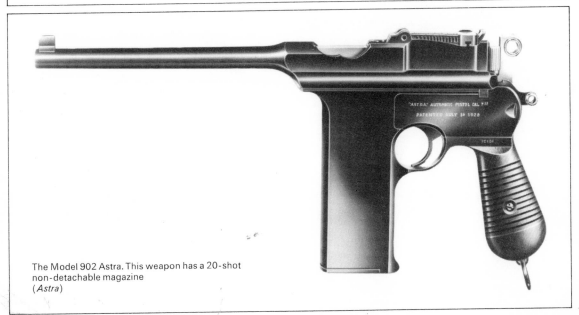

The Model 902 Astra. This weapon has a 20-shot
non-detachable magazine
(*Astra*)

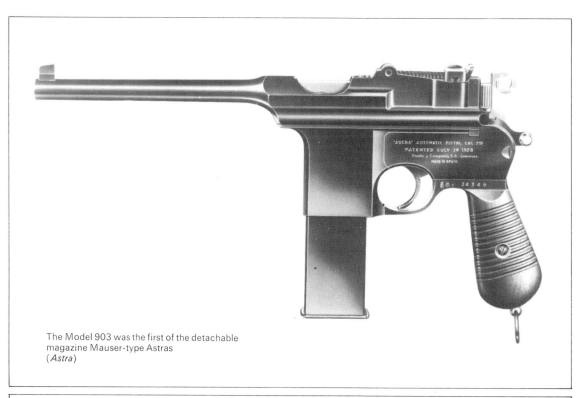

The Model 903 was the first of the detachable
magazine Mauser-type Astras
(*Astra*)

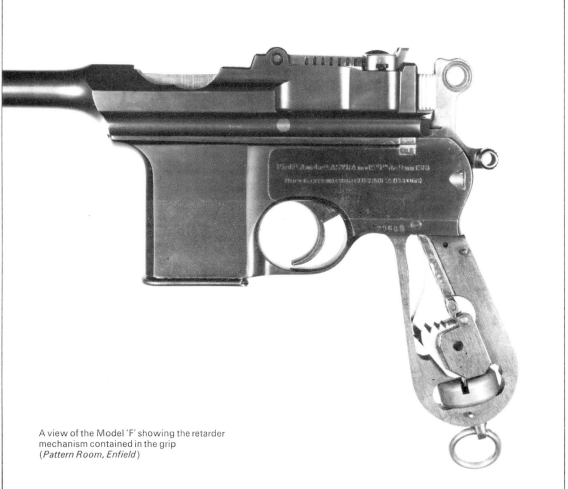

A view of the Model 'F' showing the retarder
mechanism contained in the grip
(*Pattern Room, Enfield*)

Constable (Model 5000)

In 1969 Astra announced their latest pistol which was of a totally new type as far as the Company was concerned. The pistol, the final design of which was adopted after a number of prototypes, is similar in concept to the Walther designs and features a double action trigger. The shape of the weapon departs from the 'water pistol' and Browning types as it is of a streamlined outline. It is manufactured in three calibres 9mm short (·380 ACP), 7·65 (·32 ACP) and ·22LR. The safety is mounted on the slide and not only locks the firing pin but also shields it. When the safety is applied the hammer drops on to this shield rather in the manner of the Polish Radom. The dimensions are as follows:

Overall length	6½ inches (102mm)
Barrel length	3½ inches (89mm)
Height	4½ inches (117mm)
Weight empty	25oz (720g)
Magazine capacity	·22LR—10 rounds
	·32 ACP—8 rounds
	·380 ACP—7 rounds

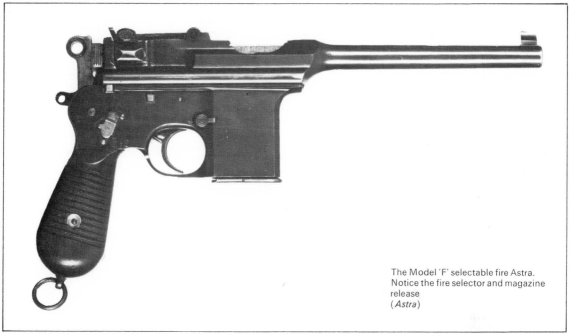

The Model 'F' selectable fire Astra. Notice the fire selector and magazine release
(*Astra*)

The Constable Sport is the latest in the Astra line of small automatic pistols. It features a double action trigger and a considerably streamlined shape. Notice the similarity with the Walther designs. This particular pistol is chambered for ·22 Long Rifle and has target sights and a long barrel
(*Astra*)

Astra Cadix

Astra decided in 1958 to announce a series of revolvers. This was the first time that the company had made other than an automatic pistol. The revolvers are all of the swing out cylinder type with a double-action trigger. A total of nine weapons are available in ·22, ·32 and ·38 special. Each calibre is available in 2, 3 and 4 inch barrels. The dimensions of the weapons are as follows:

Calibre ·22	Model 222	Model 224	Model 226	Ammunition
Overall length	163mm	227mm	278mm	·22 LR
Height	110mm	131mm	131mm	
Barrel length	51mm	102mm	153mm	
Weight without cartridges	24oz	26oz	29oz	
Cylinder capacity	9 cartridges	9 cartridges	9 cartridges	

Calibre ·32	Model 322	Model 324	Model 326	Ammunition
Overall length	163mm	227mm	278mm	·32 Long
Height	112mm	135mm	135mm	
Barrel length	51mm	102mm	153mm	
Weight without cartridges	23oz	25oz	27oz	
Cylinder capacity	6 cartridges	6 cartridges	6 cartridges	

Calibre ·38 Special	Model 382	Model 384	Model 386	Ammunition
Overall length	163mm	227mm	278mm	·38 Special S & W
Height	112mm	135mm	135mm	
Barrel length	51mm	102mm	153mm	
Weight without cartridges	22oz	24oz	24oz	
Cylinder capacity	5 cartridges	5 cartridges	5 cartridges	

The Astra 357

This revolver is the latest weapon from the Astra Company, being chambered for the ·357 Magnum cartridge. It is necessarily of heavier construction than the Cadix. It is available in a number of barrel lengths all having double action triggers, swing-out cylinders and adjustable sights. Once again as with all Astra weapons they can be had chromed, engraved, silver-plated and gold damascened. The dimensions are as follows:

Barrel lengths	76mm (3in)	102mm (4in)	152mm (6in)
Overall length	209·5mm (8¼in)	235mm (9¼in)	286mm (11¼in)
Weight	1050g	1100g	1170g
Cylinder capacity	6 cartridges	6 cartridges	6 cartridges

Astra, a leading firm among those who have made the Spanish firearms reputation second to none, continues to produce pistols which have few rivals where quality is concerned. The familiar 'Water Pistol' shape will remain as a symbol of the Astra name and, with their double action Falcon, will carry the fortunes of the company to new heights.

The Astra 357 is illustrated on page 60.

The Author must express his thanks to the Astra Company for their generous help in the completion of this Profile.

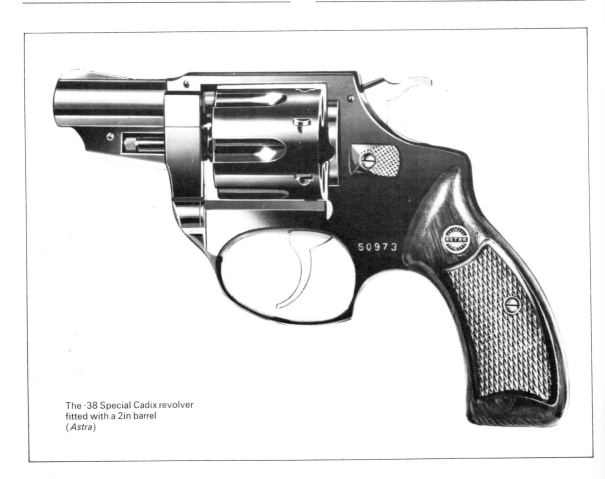

The ·38 Special Cadix revolver fitted with a 2in barrel (*Astra*)

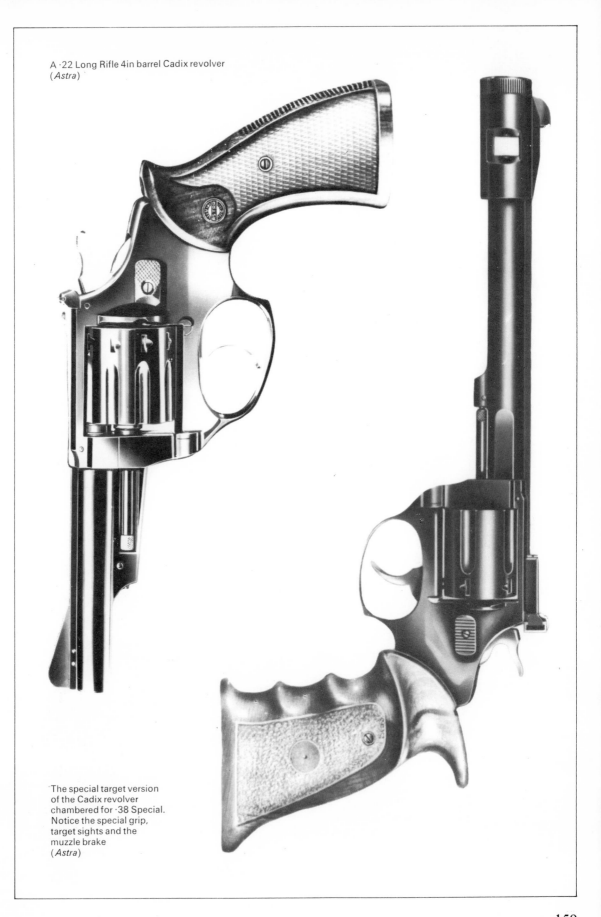

A ·22 Long Rifle 4in barrel Cadix revolver
(*Astra*)

The special target version
of the Cadix revolver
chambered for ·38 Special.
Notice the special grip,
target sights and the
muzzle brake
(*Astra*)

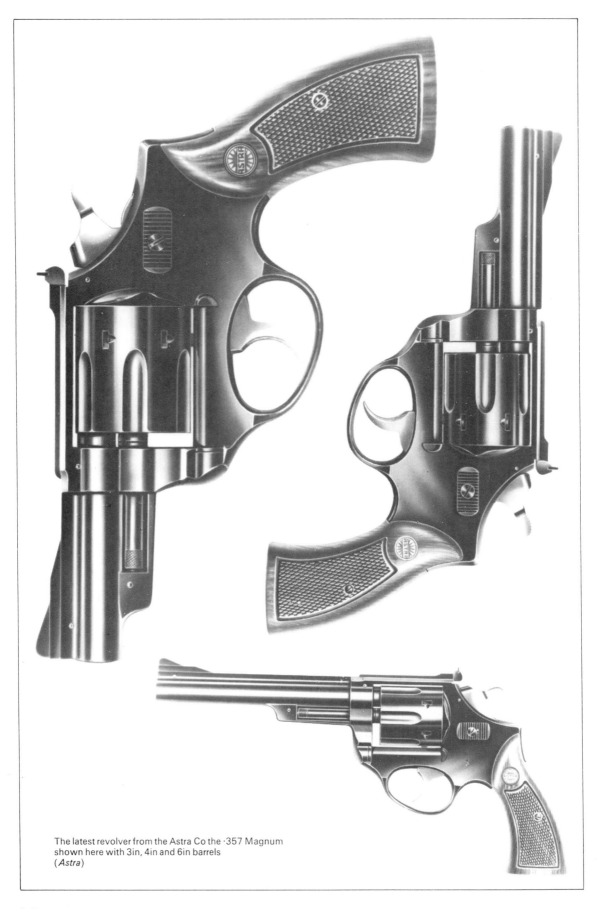

The latest revolver from the Astra Co the ·357 Magnum
shown here with 3in, 4in and 6in barrels
(*Astra*)